HOROLOGIST EXTRAORDINAIRE

Nicholas Müller

By Arlyn Rath
FNAWCC

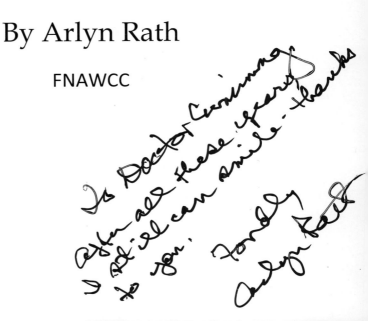

Copyright © 2011 by Arlyn Rath
All rights reserved
No part of this book may be reproduced in any form
without written permission in writing from the author.

Published by Arlyn Rath
Printed in the USA
ISBN: 978-0-615-58733-2

DEDICATION

To George C. Rath, a Fellow of the National Association of Watch & Clock Collectors, Past President of New York Chapter #2, Chairman and Co-Chairman of several Greater New York Regionals, Air Force veteran and my husband of more than 55 years, without whom this book could not have been written.

His lifelong interests in engineering, wood working and all things mechanical were the perfect background enabling him to restore and repair more than 1,800 antique clocks, virtually breathing life back into each and every one of them.

For

Allison & Peter and George & Mari

Who gave us our most precious treasures -

Our Grandchildren,

Christopher, Sarah, Bridget and Shannon

TABLE OF CONTENTS

Acknowledgements	03
Nicholas Müller	06
Jim Shawn	14
The Kroeber Connection	16
Imitation Bronzes	20
Composition Bronze & Iron Bronze	24
The Clocks and their Descriptions	26
Movements used in Müller Cases	208
Identification and Speculation	209
Restoration	214
Patent Applications	222
Index of Clocks by Name	227
Index	240
A Note from Arlyn	242
About the Author	243

INTRODUCTION

Throughout the ages, works of great beauty have been created – paintings, sculpture, furniture and accessories – which reflected the styles of the period and have shown us how people lived. Most of these treasures belonged to royalty and the very wealthy, who preserved and protected them, eventually enabling all to see and admire.

We have been fortunate to have travelled extensively throughout the world – to have seen treasures of Egypt – to be in King Tut's tomb and to see, later, the great treasures of all kinds that escorted him to his heavenly reward. We have toured palaces and museums on six continents and have seen art and furnishings of every description.

When clocks were invented, once again it was the very privileged who commissioned and owned them. Many of these were one-of-a-kind – tenderly protected over the years. We have viewed many treasures, including the great clocks in the Forbidden City at Beijing, China. These were gifts to the Emperors of China and are, of course, priceless and irreplaceable. Most of these clocks are made of bronze, gold, precious metals and valuable gemstones.

In contrast, in most of the New World (America) clocks were more architectural in design, mostly utilitarian, with cases made of wood. At first, the American clockmakers copied designs they had admired in Europe. Later, they made simple clocks for the masses. In the Nineteenth Century, many of the more expensive clocks duplicated European designs that featured statues, ornate metal cases and variations thereof.

At this time, two German born brothers immigrated to this country with dreams of fame and fortune, like so many before them. Both were artisans who began their American dream by opening a metal foundry in New York City and attempted to produce high quality clocks and accessories that appealed to the Victorian tastes.

One was a renowned sculptor, who enjoyed an excellent award-winning reputation in Europe, especially France. After only a few years in America, he returned to Europe, claiming that the Americans were uncouth and lacking in the appreciation of Fine Art. His brother, along with his family, remained in New York and became prominent within the clock-making community. He designed and made figural cases which were purchased by many of the leading horological companies of the day.

In our early days of collecting, trying to buy one of everything, inexpensively, we fell in love with some of these clocks and found ourselves gravitating more and more to these beautifully conceived and executed clock fronts. We were amazed at the lack of information about his work and determined to acquire as much as we could. We were building a wonderful collection of, what to us, reminded us of what we were seeing in Europe and on our travels.

We began to research this talented artist who happened to combine our two major areas of interest – ART and CLOCKS. This man was Nicholas Müller.

ACKNOWLEDGMENTS

This book required a great deal of research and specialized information, which I was fortunate to accumulate through the efforts of the following people.

The earliest information that I received was from Jim Shawn, of The Old Clock Museum, in Pfarr, Texas. He inspired and encouraged me in my efforts to obtain both actual clocks and information about Nicholas Müller.

This book could not have been written without the help and encouragement of two special friends - Richard Taub and Lu Sadowski.

Richard has been my computer photographic expert who greatly improved my photos and provided many of his own, scanned and brought them all into 21st Century condition. He has performed modern day miracles, photographically, that I could never have imagined and is the reason that this book has so many professional looking photos and illustrations. Lu has made important contacts and has been an unending source of information regarding the vagaries of the publishing process. She has guided me through so many possible pitfalls, always keeping me on track. Both Lu and Richard have been unending sources of encouragement and support.

My wonderful daughter, Allison Rudkin, as well as our resident computer genius, my grandson Christopher Rudkin, became my research team. They solved many enigmas regarding the meanings of the sometimes esoteric names Müller gave to many of the clocks. Chris was always available to untangle the computer glitches that I was so prone to make. He also taught me that it was not necessary to "like" the computer but rather to develop an amicable relationship with it. This peaceful co-existence enabled me to put all of my words into the "machine", as required, and have the ability to edit my words each and every step along the way. I can't thank him enough.

My sincere appreciation goes to the staff of The Library & Research Center of The National Watch & Clock Museum. They rewarded me with a flood of information - copies of original patents as well as many reprints of articles about Müller that appeared in The Jewelers' Circular and Horological Review, an extremely important source of biographical information.

Another major source of accurate information was provided by The Research Division of The American Clock and Watch Museum, located in Bristol, Connecticut. They were able to provide many original catalogs and price lists, as well as photographs. I spent two days in the lovely old museum and was amazed at the depth of the resource material available.

Many hours were spent in the Main Branch of the New York Public Library searching the census records from 1850 – 1880 as well as business records of the City – all on micro-fiche. This was daunting work since these records were recorded in various shades of ink and a variety of penmanship, making some unintelligible.

Chris Bailey, gifted author, superb researcher and recently retired curator and managing director of The American Clock and Watch Museum, was most generous in sharing information about Nicholas Müller. He provided the invaluable list of Müller's clocks (1850-1880) which he compiled and graciously offered for inclusion in this book. It was his suggestion that I explore the Müller files at The Bristol museum, which yielded much valuable information.

Many kudos to my friend and proof reader, Phyllis Taub, who spent many hours making sure that "everything is perfect". I am most appreciative of her expertise and professional attention to detail.

Tran Duy Ly has added a great service to watch and clock collectors by reproducing so many wonderful old catalogs. They were of immeasurable assistance in identifying and naming Müller's work.

My sincere thank go to Rev. James Adelmann, my pastor, for his advice on iconography that enabled me to unscramble the clues in each religious casting.

There were so many questions that arose about "The Indian Hunter a/k/a Chingachgook". I want to thank the folks at The Cooperstown Historical Society as well as fellow collectors Steve Macaluso and Martin Saltzman for their assistance.

It is with deep appreciation that I thank Bob Frishman for sharing his wonderful research on "Matthew Brady's Clock" as well as copies of Brady's famous photographs. Many thanks are in order to the late Mary Jane Strickler for acquiring Dan Ginsburg's explanation of the casting front named "Ball Players" or The Baseball Clock, and to The NAWCC for printing it in The Bulletin.

Orwell stated that writing a book was "A horrible, exhausting struggle, like a long bout of some painful illness". Mine, I fear, has been rather like an interminable gestation period of more than twenty years. Procrastination and lack of confidence in my ability to fulfill this task slowed me to a crawl.

It is my hope that I have given a presence to Nicholas Müller. He has been a part of my life for so many years, waiting to be revealed as one of the outstanding figures in American horology.

Nicholas Muller

shortcuts had to be taken. With this attitude, he and Morse achieved fame in ways that were not at first anticipated.

Nicholas married Eliza Albrecht in 1849 and their daughter, Johanna, was born the next year. She would grow up to marry clockmaker Florence Kroeber. Three of their sons also survived – William (b. 1851), Hermann (b. 1852) and Otto (b. 1856). Two other children died in their infancy.

In 1855, after his brother returned to Germany, the company was in the name of Nicholas Müller alone. He was the founder and manufacturer of spelter statues and clock cases with imitation bronze finishes. The spelter, a blend of tin and lead, was a metal that was softer and more pliable than pewter.

Since bronze was very expensive, he sought to make his products more affordable by using a different base metal – one that would show sharper and better details than iron. The pieces were then plated with bronze, so as to resemble the traditional sculptural material. This celebrated finish known as the Electrical French Bronze was introduced by Nicholas Müller, thus earning him the title "The Father of the American Bronze Industry". This plating of bronze was so heavy that it allowed for oxidation.

From 1861 – 1862 the business was located at 667 Sixth Avenue – corner of 39th Street (now part of mid-town Manhattan). The business was listed variously as founders, manufacturers, castings and bronze manufacturers. Among various addresses listed in the New York City Directory, as well as Doggets, Rodes and Wilson, from 1849 on, were 173 Greenwich Street, 23 Elm & Walker Streets, 41 Wooster Street, 68 West 49th Street & Sixth Avenue (now Rockefeller Center), 66 Beekman Street (Kroeber partnership), 8 Cortlandt Street and 117 Chambers Street.

In 1868, Nicholas entered into partnership with his future son-in-law, Florence Kroeber, under the name Müller and Kroeber, located at 68 Beekman Street (in lower Manhattan). Some clocks were produced bearing an erroneous label "Fuller" and Kroeber. This was corrected and very few labels were released to the public. The partnership failed, however, after almost two years. Both men continued separate businesses at different addresses on Cortlandt Street, with Nicholas listed as "clocks" at 8 Cortlandt Street, with his home address as 62 West 54th Street, until his death in 1873.

His widow, Eliza, continued to operate the business herself. There is little doubt that the three sons had worked with their father as apprentices (which was the practice during the Nineteenth Century). In 1875, her sons entered into the business which was then called Nicholas Müller's Sons & Co., with a partnership of Nicholas' widow, Eliza, and her sons William, then 24 years old, Herman, 23 years old and Otto the youngest at 19.

Among the patents I have examined, none were entered by Otto, only a few by William and the majority were the work of Herman, who apparently shared the creative talents of his father. The other sons, Otto and William, probably took a more active role in the production end of the business (casting, finishing and plating) all necessary to the success of the company.

Nicholas Müller's Sons & Co. manufactured many items, among them are side figures, statuettes, pitchers and side urns, bronze top figures, busts, vases, clocks, imitation marble and novelty clocks, sundry fancy goods, card plates, trays, ash stands, match safes, candlesticks, mirrors, plaques and portables, bronze lamps, thermometers, clock fronts and inkstands, according to articles in the Jewelers' Circular and Horological Review.

"Nicholas Müller had untiringly endeavored to harmonize art with the popular demand. Since his death, and the succession of his three sons, this principle has been carried out as absolutely as possible," according to another article in The Jewelers' Circular & Horological Review. "Nicholas Müller's Sons have ever endeavored to produce sterling goods both in design and finish, and to this end they have copyrighted their patterns, to prevent the demoralization of the industry due to indiscriminate copying and consequent cutting of prices. It may be remarked here that such a principle on the part of Müller's Sons is worthy of applause from jewelers as their efforts to maintain the high standards of their industry redounds to the benefit of their customers. Though they study the foreign productions, they have never copied a design of a domestic manufacturer".

Son William left the firm in 1877, only two years after he started, and died in 1884. Eliza died in 1888 and sons Otto and Herman continued. Otto left the firm in 1891 and opened another sales office at No. 83 Dearborn Street, Chicago, Illinois, while Herman continued at 17 Chambers Street, New York City. Otto had the sole agency of their goods in the West.

In 1892 the Müller Art Bronze Co. was formed, with Herman Müller as President. This succeeded Nicholas Müller's Sons & Co. There were five partners in total. Clockmaker Florence Kroeber was added as a director in 1894.

The Jewelers' Circular of February 11th, 1891 states: "One of the largest and finest lines of bronzes manufactured in the country is that of the Müller Bronze Co., whose works are in the Shiebler Building at the corner of Underhill and St. Marks' Avenues, Brooklyn, New York. All the prominent jobbers are handling them. The goods are excellent in design, workmanship and finish, and are especially adapted to the clock and jewelry trade".

This firm also failed by 1895 and was succeeded by Nicholas Müller's Son & Co, which lasted just two years, from 1895 -1897. The partners were Herman J. Müller and Max Schirrmacher. After 1897, Müller was no longer a partner and the firm was assigned to Max Mayer and ceased operation soon after.

Herman Müller remained in a business described as metal goods, plating and bronze alone until his death in 1900, after which his widow, Frances L. Müller assumed the helm. In 1918, she established The Müller Art Plating Works to continue the plating and bronze business. Still in operation in 1933, being operated by Samuel L. Lyons, it is not known if any clock cases were still manufactured.

Much of this information was provided in "Letter from America", Clocks Magazine, 1990's by Chris H. Bailey. Reprints were obtained from NAWCC

Library. Much other factual information was given in The Jewelers' Circular - October 21st, 1891.

Elzia Albright Muller (Wife)   Nicholas Muller

MULLER BRONZE CO.

Underhill & St. Marks Aves., BROOKLYN, N. Y.

MANUFACTURERS OF FINE

BRONZE ORNAMENTS FOR THE CLOCK AND JEWELRY TRADE.

ALL FIRST CLASS JOBBERS HANDLE THEM.

NEW CONCERN.   NEW GOODS.

HISTORY, No. 121.

ARTIST, No. 112.

NICHOLAS MULLER'S SONS,
No. 117 Chambers Street, NEW YORK. Manufacturers of Artistic Bronzes, Clocks, Lamps and Metal Fancy Goods. A call requested.

Lamp No. 847. Pluto.   Plaeque Clock. No. 254.   Hector, No. 324. B. P.

NICHOLAS MULLER'S SONS,
117 CHAMBERS STREET, NEW YORK.
MANUFACTURERS OF

Fine Clocks and Ornamental Bronzes.

BRASS AND BRONZE *Fancy Goods* FOR THE JEWELRY TRADE.

New Regulating Attachment (Patented).   "ROYAL," Embroidered Satin and Bronze.

JIM SHAWN

When we first began to realize that we had begun a collection of the clocks made and signed by Nicholas Müller, it was suggested that we contact Jim Shawn, of Pfarr, Texas, a former foundryman and enthusiast of Müller's clocks. I wrote to him and received an immediate response. Truly, he was the most caring, informative person I had met since joining the Association. He wasn't competing with you for the clocks you both coveted but rather encouraged and shared information he had gleaned.

He wrote us long rambling accounts, often lacking any punctuation — with sentences going on for half a page. His letters showed his passion and admiration for "Old Nicholas".

Mr. Shawn owned "The Old Clock Museum" on Preston Street in Pfarr, Texas. He stated the purpose of the Museum as follows:

"Our purpose is to preserve and display examples of early clocks from over the world. Unless something like this is done future generations will have no contact with early history other than reading and pictures. We are a non-profit, scientific and educational institution for Horological research. However, we do take contributions for the Boy Scouts and our local children's home".

We met Mr. Shawn just once, at a National Convention in Texas. He was then in a wheel chair, scouring the Mart for still another clock done by "the old boy". He passed away a few years later. We recently learned that the Museum in Texas has been closed and the clocks sent to auction. Fortunately, I was able to obtain a few that we had not previously owned.

(Postcard of Old Clock Museum, Pharr, Texas – now closed.)

I have most of the letters he sent us, his lists and a request that, since we live in the New York area, I should do local research and let people know how truly exceptional Nicholas Müller was. I will not forget him and am sure that he would be "real pleased that I got around to it".

THE KROEBER CONNECTION

Johanna (Muller) Kroeber, daughter of Nicholas Muller and wife of Florence Kroeber, taken in 1881 at the age of 32.

Florence Kroeber taken in 1881 at age 41.

Much of the information in this chapter was obtained from the article "Florence Kroeber the Great Horological Orchestrator" by Chris Bailey.

Florenz Friedrich Martin Kroeber was born on June 7th, 1840 in the city of Paderborn, Westphalia, Germany. The Kroeber family left Cologne, where they resided at the time, and immigrated to America in the spring of 1850. Their four young sons accompanied them and the family settled in New York City. Florence (his name was Anglicized) was raised in the German area of New York.

He did not attend formal school until he was 16 and, as the oldest son, he was expected to help support the family by taking jobs. When his father died, Florence was employed by the firm of Owen & Clark, merchandisers of clocks at 25 John Street.

At first he was a bookkeeper but soon became interested in other aspects of the clock business. Owen & Clark dissolved their business relationship in 1864. Owen went to work with William L. Gilbert, but Owen and Kroeber continued to work together and Kroeber often used Owen's designs for walnut parlor clocks.

It was surprising to me, after reading his biographical material, to learn that Kroeber was not a skilled movement maker, as I had previously believed, but rather a marketer of cases designed by him using movements acquired from others.

"In 1868, Florence Kroeber went into partnership with Nicholas Müller, a manufacturer of cast metal clock cases", according to Chris Bailey," and they opened a store at 66 Beekman Street, for about a year, primarily to sell home furnishings. This firm was in addition to the continuing business each separately ran.

"Some clocks were marketed by the firm of Müller & Kroeber though, curiously, many of these carry a misprinted label stating "Fuller & Kroeber" as the manufacturer. This year Kroeber also acted as an agent for the Gilbert Manufacturing Company, located at 12 Cortlandt Street".

In 1870 Kroeber married Johanna, the eldest child of Nicholas and Eliza Müller, (Nicholas having been his former business partner). For the first few years, they lived in Hoboken, New Jersey, where his brother lived. In 1878, they relocated to Lower Manhattan and purchased a brownstone at 32 East 78th Street (off Fifth Avenue at Central Park.) Brownstones are generally 15, 20 or 25 feet wide and attached at both sides. Interestingly enough, these three and four story homes still stand graciously throughout many areas of New York City and those in Kroeber's immediate neighborhood sell for about 5 to 10 million dollars or more, if available at all.

Four children survived – Alfred (1876-1960) who studied anthropology at Columbia University and became a professor of Anthropology at The University of California – Edward (1878-1899) single – Johanna (1880-1969) studies biology at Bryn Mawr College and worked at The American Museum of Natural History and helped establish The Crippled Children's Hospital in NYC – and Elsbeth (1882-1969) attended Barnard- remained single and became an assistant principal in New York City Schools.

The family was prosperous (as may be seen by the fine schools the children attended) due to the success of the clock business. Alfred worked in his father's clock case shop at one point and was said to be skilled at cabinet work.

As early as the late 1860's Kroeber was purchasing some American movements from Connecticut makers – for which he manufactured clock cases.

In some ways, Kroeber's and Müller's business lives paralleled one another. Neither of them manufactured the actual clock movements, but both were case manufacturers. After the death of Nicholas, his sons did sell some complete clocks with the movements marked "N. Müller & Sons", however. Perhaps Kroeber is better known because he sold fully assembled clocks (retail) in his own cases and purchased movements. The clocks were then marketed under his own name. Müller was more of a wholesaler; some often marketed using the movement maker's name.

"E. Ingraham Co. of Bristol Conn. on March 29th, 1878, quoted a resolution of The Association about Kroeber, allowing him to continue "fitting up clocks". Besides Ingraham, the other movements that were known to be used by Kroeber were Seth Thomas, Laporte Hubbell, Ansonia and most likely E. N. Welch, as well as New Haven and William Gilbert Clock Co."

Cast metal cases also made up a great part of the clocks he listed as his own, yet these cases were largely if not totally supplied by Nicholas Müller and his successor Müller firms and were without the Müller name on the case. This was also done by other companies using Müller cases. It has been suggested that Ansonia and Seth Thomas metal clocks used Müller cases.

At 65 years of age, Kroeber was financially ruined and his health was beginning to fail from tuberculosis. He died on May 16th, 1911.

There was until recently gender confusion. According to Chris Bailey, The New York Times carried the following obituary: KROEBER – on May 16, 1911, Florence Kroeber in HER 71st Year. Funeral Private.

Until a few decades ago, his clocks were presumed to have been made by a woman. A friend of mine, Norma Doob, an enthusiastic collector, was researching a book which she planned to call "The First Woman Clockmaker." She was extremely disappointed, upon learning that SHE was a HE.

His widow (Nicholas Müller's daughter) died in 1933 – aged 84 – and was interred in the family plot in the magnificent Greenwood Cemetery, Brooklyn, New York. We recently took a bus tour to this beautiful place of her internment, near the likes of Currier and Ives, Louis Comfort Tiffany and thousands of other notables.

Although the legal partnership of Müller and Kroeber was short-lived, the relationship seems to have continued, through familial ties, business locations and co-dependence. Kroeber needed the genius of Müller's artistry and Müller needed the continuing source of revenue provided by Kroeber's use of his sculptural masterpieces.

Both men contributed mightily to the burgeoning clock business in the United States and are to be commended for their ingenuity.

IMITATION BRONZES

THEIR HISTORY AND THE METHODS OF MANUFACTURE

This article appeared in NAWCC Bulletin # 252, February 1988 and was reprinted from The Keystone, September, 1892.

What are imitation bronzes? Is a hard question, for there immediately arises the further question. In what respect are they imitation, as imitation is so wide a term? An imitation of an article may be an imitation of its substance, or of its looks, or of its taste, or of half a dozen different qualities. Again, it depends upon what the advantages of the real article are, whether they can be really imitated to good purpose, for there are some things, even if they are imitated so as to appear precisely the same as the article which they are to replace, would have but little value. Take a diamond, for instance. If it is an imitation which, as far as looks are concerned, could not be distinguished from the original, but which was known to be an imitation, it would not be worth anything, compared with the original; and this applies to all articles which are sought after, for their rarity mainly – such as a very rare copy of a book. A very rare copy of the Bible, written out by hand hundreds of years ago, will bring much more than the most beautifully printed one of modern times; still, hardly anyone will deny that, for actual use, the print of today is equal to the best hand-written book of former times, while it has the great advantage of superior cheapness.

But, leaving aside this question of genuineness, independent of qualities, the next question is, - What qualities do we wish to imitate – essential qualities? If we wish to imitate a thing so as to be useful, all we really care for, as a rule, are the essential qualities. If we wish to imitate it, for the purpose of deceit, we will also try to imitate the accidental qualities. Hence, in imitation bronzes, which are copies of beautiful objects, ordinarily made in real bronze, we really reproduce a perfect article for our own use, if we imitate the essential qualities; but inasmuch as the general public wish to have their friends believe that they have a higher-priced article than it really is, the dealer must endeavor also to imitate the accidental qualities.

This brings us still further to consider, what are the essential qualities which we intend to imitate, and which are the accidental qualities? Among then essential qualities, we may mention beauty of form, which all sculptors aim at in either bronze or marble; and which is more perfectly brought out in sculpture than in painting; coloring, which will bring out this beauty. It will be most proper to consider first the essential qualities, for this will enable us to tell how far imitation bronze fulfilled the purposes of bronzes; and when we speak of imitation bronzes, we have all along understood this term to mean, in modern times, electro-imitation bronze. But now to the essential qualities. Naturally, first of all, comes beauty of form, which all sculptors aim at, and which beauty of form is more perfectly brought out in sculpture than in painting, for reasons so well known that they need not be explained. While this beauty of form is the most essential quality, the bronze coloring is also essential, as it is often needed to bring out the beauty of form. Next to these essential artistic qualities is another very important quality – strength – which renders bronze superior, in the eyes of many to marble, not to speak of imitations of marble or porcelain, or clay, etc. It will be noticed that in all of these essential qualities (excepting to a slight degree in the quality of strength), the electro-imitation bronze fulfills the requirements as well as the real bronze.

But how about the accidental qualities? It might be supposed that, inasmuch as they are accidental, the electro-imitation bronze would not possess them as fully as the real bronze would; and still, in the eyes of many, they play a very important role. First of all comes the property of heaviness which can also be given to electro-imitation bronze; but as it would serve no purpose but that of deceit, it is generally not given to the imitation bronzes, for the lighter and thinner a bronze is cast, the more perfect it will be apt to be. Another accidental quality is the hardness of the real bronze and consequent difficulty to work, which makes the real bronze rarer, and which is one of the great reasons for the attempt to make cheap substitutes.

From these two standpoints it will be seen that the electro-imitation bronzes will more and more occupy the field of real bronzes, as in most cases they will answer the purpose as well as the real. But what does history tell us of imitation bronzes? Many people think that imitation bronzes are only a product of our modern world; but to anyone who knows that the world is pretty much now as it always was, this will seem strange, and a little research will show that even in ancient times there were imitations of real bronze made, which can even now be seen in many museums of Europe, even in many of the smaller museums of the small, old towns of Northern Europe, which were occupied by Rome – such as Mayence, etc. Examining these specimens, we will readily see that the main reason why imitation bronzes were not more widely scattered was that they could not possess all the essential qualities of bronze so well as our modern electro-bronze, because they were made of much inferior material, and very frequently simply painted over. They were made out of lead, wood, tin and all sorts of things. This is reason sufficient to show why imitation bronzes did not flourish much until about the middle of this century, independent of the fact that it is only since comparatively recent years that more than a small proportion of people have had any spare means for the gratification of their artistic taste. But outside of this, the main cause of the great development of electro-imitation bronzes has been the discovery and improvements in zinc-casting, in addition to another cause, which we will presently speak of more at length, and that is electro-plating. Although zinc had been known for quite a while, it had not been practically used to any great extent until after 1840, when improvements were first made, and was first practically cast in Berlin for large monumental work about the year 1844. From there its use spread quite rapidly, although it had been experimented on for some years previous to this; and, in fact, the beginning of the art was almost as early in America as in Europe, as we shall see later.

Zinc, which is the basis of the better electro-imitation bronze, is a metal which flows so sharply that it well takes the place of bronze, while at the same time, its great fluidity renders it much more easy to work, and it is also, fortunately, considerably cheaper. But the main cause of the development of imitation bronzes, which before the middle of this century had always to be colored virtually by painting, was the introduction of the art of electro-plating. As most people know, as the word signifies, this was at first applied to the deposition of silver by electricity, but soon paved the way to the electro deposition of copper on a practical scale. The electro deposition of alloys, such as bronze, brass, etc., naturally followed, but was brought out about as early in America as in Europe, although the men who first introduced these arts in America received most of their training, and the seeds from which their thoughts came, from European sources. It was first practically introduced in this country by Nicholas Müller, who made quite a study of it, theoretically as well as practically, in order to make a success of imitation bronzes, which he thought would be a great medium for introducing higher art and a better knowledge of sculpture among the populace; for it was he who, with his brother, the eminent sculptor, Karl Müller, made the first imitation bronze in the United States, and was among the first to widely introduce zinc-castings from metal moulds, although it is but just to say that probably the first one to introduce the art of casting zinc in America, and one of the first, in fact, to practice zinc-casting on a larger scale throughout the world, was Mr. Seelig, whose name still appears in the firm of N. J. Seelig & Co., Brooklyn, E.D. They, however, generally confined themselves to large work for out-of-doors, which was not electro-plated, and therefore not strictly imitation bronze, while Nicholas Müller from the very first, endeavored to make goods which should be like real bronzes, or at least like the French imitation of real bronze, or what are called French bronzes.

Naturally our pride in the reflection that America, which is so young in experience, should be as old in the trade of imitation bronzes as Europe, is, if anything, brightened, by the circumstance that the cause of this was the fact that the great middle class were earlier able in this country to gratify their tastes for articles of beauty than the mass of the people in Europe; and so even in this sketch of imitation bronzes, we come to recognizing the superiority of our advantages, just as the ancients well said, "All roads lead to Rome".

COMPOSITION BRONZE AND IRON BRONZE

For years, people who collected the clocks of Nicholas Müller insisted that any case that was iron was an early reproduction. (A magnet will be attracted to iron – an easy test.) I was frankly dismayed to find that a few of our clocks are iron and therefore not original.

To quote Jim Shawn, " Don't say old man Müller used cast iron he might kick the dirt out of his face and come out after you a magnet will not stick to any of them", (from a letter to Stacy Wood, dated February 13th, 1984.)

Recently, I was in touch with Chris Bailey, a noted author of horological literature as well as the recently retired curator of The American Clock and Watch Museum, a real gem of a museum in Bristol, Connecticut. He was very kind to send me some Müller information and to suggest that I visit Bristol, as there is quite a bit of information about Müller and his clocks to be found there.

An appointment was made to meet with Mary Jane Dapkus, then the new Assistant Curator of the Museum, who provided much information that the Museum has amassed, such as genealogy, photographs, 19th century price lists and catalogs, both original and copies. While she was duplicating some of the documents for me, I looked through a large folder of data for the second then the third time until something caught my eye in some reprints of the 1875 Waterbury Clock Company price list. There were several column s entitled 1 day Iron Bronzes and 8 day Iron Bronzes. Within the list were the familiar names that Müller used in the same basic time frame.

Because my interest was so piqued, I returned two weeks later and went through stacks of catalogs from 1845 – 1895, and was able to establish identities for some of my unmarked, suspected Müllers. Some are still an enigma.

There was a folder entitled "Fuller & Kroeber", which contained misprinted labels, catalogs and price lists. Sure enough, in the Fuller & Kroeber price list, dated September, 1866, when Müller partnered briefly with his future son-in-law, Florence Kroeber, were the same references to "Iron Bronze" as well as "Composition Bronze". This confirms that Müller did actually make and market Iron castings, which were thereafter bronze plated, in the same manner as were the composition castings.

Cost was obviously the motive. The results were almost the same. Our own iron castings are smoother, with fewer details in the product. As mentioned earlier, "the pewter-like, spelter-like" blend of tin and lead plus "other ingredients" actually made a clearer, cleaner, more detailed casting. Where finances are concerned however, the iron castings sold for seventy-five cents to almost two dollars less — in the value of the money of the time, a buyer could save a great deal of money for the almost identical looking item.

Here you will find a copy of a price list that shows the Iron bronze one and eight day castings. All of the "Iron Bronze" examples seem to have been made during the earlier production years of the company, during Nicholas' lifetime.

WEBSTER

Number:	3
Height:	15"
Movement:	8 day time & strike
Catalogs:	1853 – 1867
Patent:	A.P.

We show our example in the base pewter-like alloy – no plating or painting – just a simple sealer. This model is the lowest number used on any clock we have found. It is a very plain, uninteresting case. It was offered by Chauncey Jerome in 1852 (New Haven, Conn.) and was still offered by the Waterbury Clock Co. of Waterbury, Ct. in 1867.

    Müller started numbering his work but appears to have mixed items in his sequential numbering system, (clocks, inkwells and other commercial items.) Clocks seem to have all been numbered sequentially through #275, with other products interspersed. Our case has a T.S. Sperry, American Clock Mfg. label inside the case.

    Generally, Müller's clock cases were representational – that is, the appearance of the clocks was almost always reflected in the titles given them. In this model, one of the earliest, perhaps the first clock case he made, we are given the casting and its name. In its simplicity, it could be interpreted as being book shaped. Working from that thought and factoring in the date of manufacture (early 1850's), it could be assumed to commemorate Noah Webster's issuance of The Dictionary of the English language (1830-1840). The Merriam Webster Thesaurus followed in 1850, its acceptance as a resource for students began.

Webster

SCROLL

Number:	11
Height:	14 ½"
Movement:	One day – G. S. Lovell
Patent:	Applied for 1854 – Patented May 10, 1877
Catalogs:	1865 – 1876
Prices:	Composition bronze - $4.75, Iron Bronze $4.25

By definition, a scroll is anything having the form of a partly or loosely unrolled sheet of paper. This model shows scrolls on many parts of the case. The casting is not meticulously carved but rather more primitive – not as artistically made as later models.

Our case is made of iron, which is more difficult to work with than the pewter alloy. It is slightly more ornate and interesting than "Webster".

American Clock Co., in their 1874 catalog offered this model in both composition and iron bronze, the iron being 50 cents cheaper. Since both were bronze plated, the customer had a choice – the iron casting being less defined but similar in appearance. Clocks with Müller cast fronts were offered at their New York City outlet for many clock firms.

Scroll

BIRDS AND CUPIDS

Number: XII (unusual)

Height: 22"

Movement: 8 day time & strike

Patent: Unknown

This casting is marked under the bezel with Roman numerals – such numbering is the only example we have found. The two bezels show the time dial at the top and the movement of the pendulum at the bottom.

The casting depicts two putti (or cupids) at the base of the one piece front. Some element s of the design were cast separately and affixed to the front. It is similar to others using grapes, grape leaves, flowers and birds in the design.

A label on the back of the case reads:

> Martin Bennett – Watchmaker & Jeweler
>
> Brooklyn, NY
>
> Purchased March 29, 1895
>
> Warranted for one year $1.25

This clock could have been a special order as it, like the "Policeman", has numbers that are not consistent with Müller's work.

Birds and Cupids

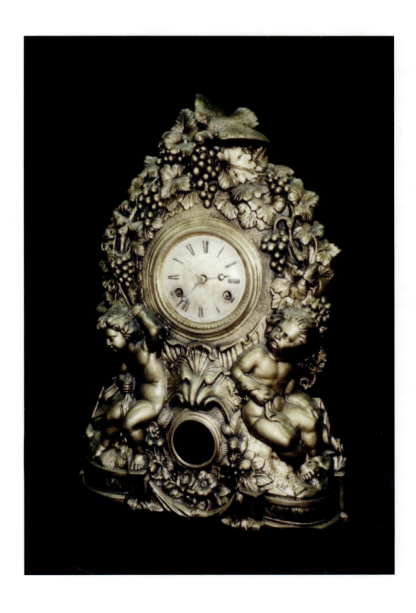

DRAGON

Number:	12
Height:	15 ½"
Movement:	30 hour time & strike
Catalogs:	1867 – 1876
Patent:	A.P.
Prices:	1866 "Fuller" & Kroeber list – one day bronze - $5.25
	1875 Waterbury Clock Co. list – composition bronze - $4.75

Our case is a one piece front with two bezels. It shows clear details and has been cast in composition bronze. The lion head at the top was a typical motif of the 19th century. Twin winged dragons are outward facing at the lower part of the case. It is decorated with the usual flowers, scrolls and acanthus leaves.

The dragon is a mythological monster, usually represented as a large reptile with wings and claws, breathing out fire and smoke. He is a legendary creature, typically with serpentine or otherwise reptilian traits that feature in the myths of many cultures. He may also be found on many coats of arms worldwide.

Dragon

GOTHIC

Number:	19
Height:	19"
Movement:	8 day time & strike
Catalogs:	1858 – 1876
Patent:	A. P.
Prices:	1874 – 8 day $7.25 One day $6.00

    The Müller mark is found under the bottom bezel. The movement in this example is U. S. Clock Co., NY, USA, but it was also offered by C. Jerome. This is one of the earliest – an interior label reads Owen E. Clark, American Clock Manufacturers, No 25 John Street, New York.

    This case is characteristic of Gothic architecture. Exteriors are frequently dominated by twin towers. Façades were pierced by entrance portals often lavishly decorated with sculpture. Additional towers frequently rose above the crossing and the arms of the transept which often had entrance portals and sculpture of their own. The upper part of the edifice was a profusion of flying buttresses and pinnacles. Gothic ribbing served to delineate the vaults with a skeletal web. Müller managed to incorporate many of the characteristics of this style.

    In the "Fuller" & Kroeber price list, Gothic was offered in one day bronze for $5.50 and one day iron bronze for $4.50 in 1866.

Gothic

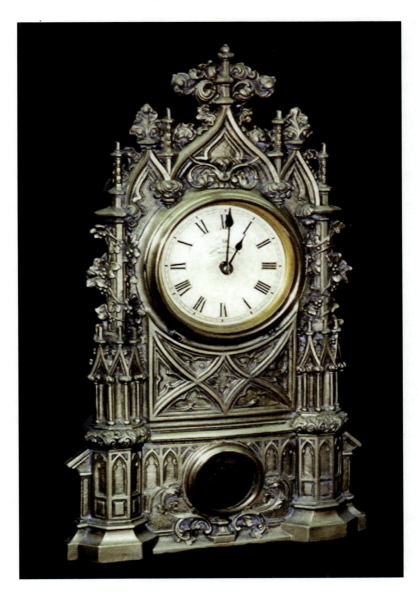

LION HEAD

Number:	30
Height:	15"
Movement:	30 hours
Catalogs:	1858 - 1876
Patent:	A. P.
Prices:	"Fuller & Kroeber 1866 – one day bronze $5.25
	One day iron bronze - $4.25
	1875 Waterbury – 8 day composition bronze - $6.00
	8 day iron bronze - $5.50

This casting shows two lions, one on either side of the bottom pendulum opening. The case is embellished with garlands and shows a human head at the top. Once again, the iron model will not be as sharp and clear as the composition bronze but, in most economies, price often dictates choice. Once again, the listing of both composition bronze and iron bronze by two different companies, particularly since one is Müller's own company, lends more credence to the fact that Müller did use iron in his work.

    The lion is a magnificent animal who appears as a symbol of power, courage and nobility on family crests, coats of arms and national flags in many civilizations. Lions are the world's most sociable felines, and work cooperatively with their pride mates. It is the lioness who stalks and kills the prey, dragging the carcass back to the pride, where the lion, alone, eats as much and the best of the offerings before allowing the "wives and kids" to partake of the leavings. It has been said that The lion is "King of the Jungle", but it is the lioness who puts the food on the table.

Lion Head

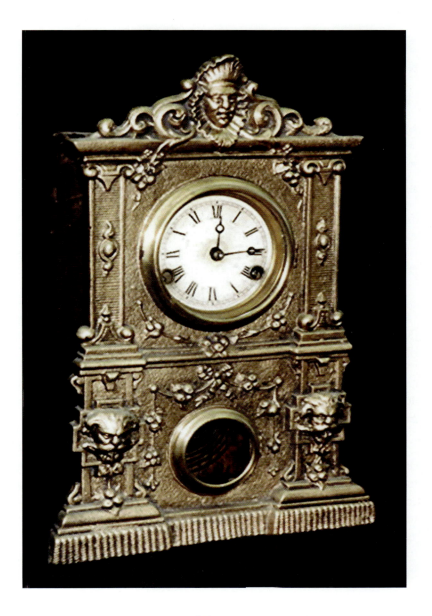

MOUSTACHE

(later listed as No. 34)

Number:	34
Height:	13"
Movement:	30 Hour
Listed:	1858 – 1876
Price:	1874 & 75 - $3.50

This clock has a one piece front with two bezels – some elements were cast and then applied to the front, the old man's head being one of them. Our example has used an unusual movement. The alarm wheel may be seen in the center of the scalloped cut out dial.

    This is a whimsical clock, showing the old man's mustache stretched from side to side across the case. Once again, Müller was merchandising his designs – the men of the middle to late 19th century did "sport" mustaches of many sizes and shapes.

    In the mid nineteenth century the stylish young man wore a sack suit, derby hat and turned down collar. He had a full beard, waxed mustache and his hair was parted and combed back.

    I have a photograph of my maternal great grandfather similarly dressed, but without a beard. He looked like a "dandy" and surely must have cut quite a figure for the young girls in Westerly, Rhode Island.

Moustache

ADAM AND EVE

Number:	35
Height:	18"
Movement:	8 day time & strike
Patent:	A.P. 1859 – stamped Patent Pending
Catalog:	1858

      This is an unusual early case, in that the figures are separate molds affixed on wrap-around sides. It is ornate for the period and features metal sides and top. The only catalog reference I was able to find was a listing in the New Haven catalog of 1858.

      A Putti head in a scallop shell is prominent at the top of the case. Flower festoons decorate the motif. Adam and Eve appear to be emerging from the foliage and vegetation. It is the earliest example of a religious theme that I have found. Later on the company introduced "The Evangelists" "Peter and Paul" and "Cathedral". Once again Müller reached out to satisfy the interests of his market.

      The story of Adam and Eve forms the basis for Christian doctrines of sin.   It is sometimes referred to as "the world's oldest love story".

Adam and Eve

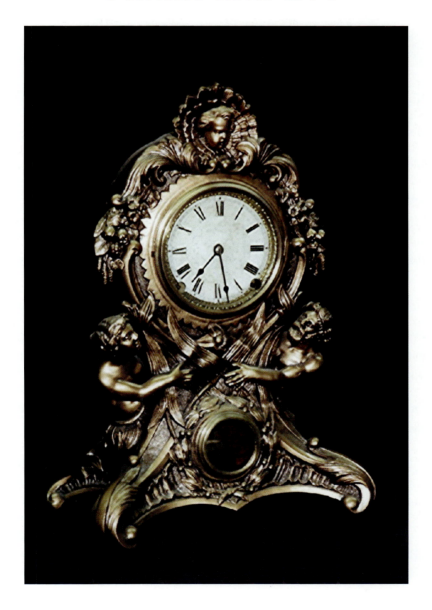

LADY

(Occasionally called "Lady Lever")

Number:	36
Height:	13"
Movement:	Both 8 day and 30 hour made with Terry movements
Catalogs:	1969 – 1876
Patent:	1867
Prices:	Composition bronze – 1 day time - $6.50, 1 day t & s $7.00

This is an unusually interesting smaller clock using many different elements added to the case, especially on the top part of the case. It is listed in the Terry catalogs and featured their very special lever movement.

This is a very desirable model due for the most part to the Terry movement. Müller provided the cases and designs for several similar small clocks for Terry, ("Boy and Dog" and "Innocence", for example).

Attitude, poise, elegance of speech, posture and self confidence are traits that define a lady and make her a perfect woman. A lady is feminine but not weak.

If a man is expected to behave like a gentleman, then it is only fitting that he has a lady by his side.

Lady

EVANGELIST

Number:	38
Height:	20"
Movement:	8 day time & strike
Patent:	A. P.
Catalogs:	1858 – 1876
Prices:	1874 – one day - $5.50 - 8 day - $8.75

    This clock, an American Clock Mfg. product, features a Gothic Cathedral shaped case. Two seated, robed, bearded men grace either side of the case. One holds a book and the other a feather quill in his right hand and a book in his left.

    Matthew, Mark, Luke and John are usually known as the Evangelists. They wrote the four Gospels known as The Gospel of Matthew, etc. Luke is known as the first iconographer. By definition, Iconology is the study of the meaning of works of visual art through the analysis of subject matter, symbolism, imagery, style, medium and historical context.

    In attempting to identify the men shown on this clock, it would seem that the man holding the quill pen would be Luke. My own guess would be that the other man depicted is Matthew, simply because Muller made another case called "Peter & Paul". This way, he covered all four of the Evangelists on these two cases.

    Our clock is marked – T. S. Sperry, 26 John Street, N. York. The "Fuller" & Kroeber price list of September, 1866, lists the one day composition bronze at $5.75 and the eight day composition bronze at $8.25. The Waterbury 1875 catalog lists a one day Iron Bronze at $4.75.

Evangelist

PETER AND PAUL

Number:	44
Height:	20 ½"
Movement:	8 day time & strike
Catalogs:	1858 – 1876
Patent:	1856
Prices:	From $6.75 to $8.75

    This imposing Gothic shaped case depicts centrally located church windows. The two Apostles are robed and bearded and shown standing. If we apply our iconographical information we can easily identify the man at the right as Peter, who is holding "The Key to Heaven". The man at the left is then Paul, holding the book, by process of elimination.

    Gothic arches and elements comprise the case under the upper bezel. We have found two examples – one with an N. Pomeroy movement and the other by Gilbert Mfg. Co. It is unknown whether any of Müller's clocks were used exclusively by one or two movement makers.

    In the 1875 Waterbury price list, an eight day Iron Bronze model was $6.75 and the eight day time & strike composition bronze was $8.75. In the "Fuller" and Kroeber price list of 1866, the eight day bronze was $8.75.

Peter and Paul

JUNO - SMALL

Number:	47
Height:	16" (small size)
Movement:	30 hours
Patent:	1867
Catalogs:	1858 – 1876
Price:	One day - $5.75

The small sized version of this model is numbered with a lower number than the full sized, eight day model. Perhaps the demand was great and it was decided that a more imposing size was appropriate. This is a one-piece, two bezel front. It was a very popular design, used by several companies in both sizes.

As to the name, Juno was a Roman goddess, with Hera as her Greek counterpart. Hera was the queen of the Gods – wife of Zeus and the goddess of marriage. In this casting she is shown with a peacock. This leads us to Aesop's Fables. The story is told in the listing of the large Juno - number 51.

Juno (small)

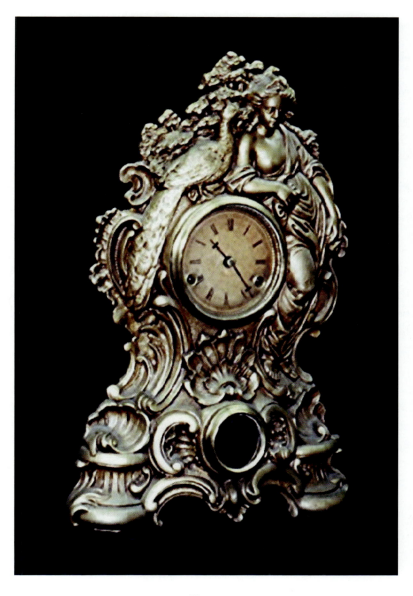

CUPID

Number:	49
Height:	19" (large version)
Movement:	8 day time & strike
Patent:	1857
Catalogs:	1858 – 1876
Price:	1874 - $9.00

     This is probably one of the most popular models sold during the last half of the 19th century. We have seen more examples of this clock, in all three forms, than we have any other. Victorians seemed to dote on cherubs or "Putti". The clock shown is a one piece front with two bezels. It contains a Jerome eight day time & strike movement, although we have seen other movements by various makers.

   "Cupid" was also offered in two thirty hour versions, as may be seen in the listing of the small "Cupid" #57. The large front was offered in both composition bronze at $9.00 and the reduced price Iron Bronze at $6.50, according to the "Fuller and Kroeber" price list of 1866.

Cupid

JUNO

Number:	51
Height:	19" (Large size)
Movement:	8 day time & strike
Patent:	1867
Catalogs:	1858 – 1876
Price:	$8.25 in 1874 catalog

Unless you carefully study the two models side by side, they appear to be exactly the same in every way except size. Take time to notice the subtle as well as the obvious differences. The large case is much more ornately decorated than the small, although they appear to be identical. Our example has a Jerome movement.

The Story of the Peacock and Juno

The peacock made a complaint to Juno that, while the nightingale pleased every ear with his song, he himself no sooner opened his mouth than he became a laughingstock to all who heard him. The Goddess, to console him said, "But you far excel in beauty and in size. The splendor of the emerald shines in your neck and you unfold a tail gorgeous with painted plumage." "But for what purpose have I", said the bird, "this dumb beauty so long as I am surpassed in song?" "The lot of each," replied Juno, "has been assigned by the will of the Fates – to thee, beauty; to the eagle, strength; to the nightingale, song; to the raven favorable, and to the crow, unfavorable auguries. These are all contented with the endowments allotted to them."

(Translated by George Fyler Townsend)

Juno

PARLOR

Number:	unknown
Height:	10"
Movement:	8 day time & strike
Catalogs:	1869 – 1876
Price:	1874 - $8.75

      This case has a flat top and is different from other Müllers in its utter simplicity.

      Although it was offered in several catalogs while Nicholas was still alive, it would appear to have been the work of someone else, possibly one of his sons. The incised designs on the case are used later in the company's production lines, after the death of the patriarch.

      A parlor is defined as a room for the reception and entertainment of visitors to one's home. At the conclusion of these greetings, the men would remain in the parlor to talk. At that time, obviously, it was expected that the women would then get to work.

Parlor

LEATHER STOCKINGS

Number:	52
Height:	20 ¼"
Movement:	8 day time & strike
Catalog:	1858
Patent:	1856
Prices:	$6.75 - $8.75

This front depicts one of James Fenimore Cooper's novels about the American frontier, with an eagle at top, trellising at sides and dog and frontiersman at base. This model contains a Waterbury Clock Co. movement.

James Fenimore Cooper (1789 – 1851), an American novelist, wrote the Leatherstocking Tales in five novels. Natty Bumpo, known as Hawkeye, a child of white parents, raised by Native Americans, was the major character in all five novels. He is shown in a coonskin cap, carrying a rifle. In a later novel, The Indian Hunter (or Chingachgook) also is immortalized as another of Cooper's characters in the same series.

In 1866, the price was $8.75 for composition bronze. In 1875, the same model was offered in an eight day time and strike movement in Iron Bronze for $6.75. No other finish was offered. Once again, the company offered choices.

Leather Stockings

EAGLE

Number:	54
Height:	18 ½"
Movement:	8 day time & strike
Catalogs:	1858 – 1876
Patent:	A.P.
Prices:	1866 – 8 day comp. bronze $9.00
	Iron Bronze $7.25 Waterbury list

A truly historical flat front two bezel clock, this prompted Jim Shawn to write, eloquently, the following in NAWCC Bulletin, October 1985, # 238, Volume XXVII No. 1.

"The average collector looks down on these little cast front clocks simply because, as a rule, they have two or more coats of barn paint smeared over a layer of dirt which all but does away with the fine details of the casting. But where, I would like to ask, are we going to find the early history of our country standing out in bold relief on a single clock front, even on the finest of our wooden cased clocks?

"From the bottom to top, we first see the early transportation of this country; next the articles of war; then the eagle for protection; on both sides agriculture; on the right industry and the left the medical profession. Now please tell me, where are we going to find such blatant symbols of our history, even on our best Howard Banjo case?"

The article is called "Cast Clock Cases by Nicholas Müller & Sons" by Jim Shawn. Bulletin #238 – page 564.

Eagle

CUPID

Number:	57
Height:	15 ½" (small size)
Catalogs:	1858 – 1876
Patent:	1856
Movement:	One day time & strike and 8 day time & strike
Prices:	One day $6.50 Eight day $7.75

    This is a small model of a popular subject, offered with both one and eight day movements. It was also made with a more inexpensive alarm clock style movement. This model had the bottom bezel opening eliminated in favor of a foliage form. A bezel here is unnecessary due to the lack of a pendulum.

    You may see here an exact replica of the large sized "Cupid", unlike the subtle differences in the large and small "Juno". In the accompanying pictures it is easy to see the differences both on the front and the back of the iron bronze model. The modification appears to have been done prior to the casting process. It is likely that, in his quest for offering some lower priced clocks, Müller tried a different approach, using a much simpler, less costly movement. He did use iron, plated with bronze in many of his other works, but with a smaller strap type, pendulum run movement. This new movement would have been a very inexpensive addition to his line.

Cupid

BIRDS

Number:	59
Height:	21"
Catalogs:	1858 – 1875
Patent:	1857
Movement:	8 day time & strike
Price:	1875 - $9.25

This is a large, attractive case decorated with foliage – buds, cones, decorative leaves and trellis with two separately cast birds attached to either side of the lower bezel.

Our model is signed under the lower bezel and marked A. P. (Patent Applied For). There are two oval friezes at the base, as well as classical figures, flowers and buds below. Price was in an 1866 Waterbury catalog.

Birds are always with us. Noah was given hope of salvation by a bird. Egyptians made important decisions by auguring birds. Carrier pigeons saved lives in World War I. My recollections of birds will always include accompanying my Kindergarteners on bird watching trips in a local field, armed with hand drawn tally sheets and toilet paper roll tube binoculars.

It seems certain that the New Yorkers of the mid 19th century celebrated the sight of the first robin of spring, after a long, cold winter. Birds are deserving of our conservation efforts. They are truly worthy of commemorating, as Müller has done in this casting.

Birds

CHERUB AND GRAPES

Number:	60
Height:	19"
Movement:	8 day time & strike
Patent:	A. P.

      This large, one piece casting with two bezels is clearly marked on our case with Müller's name, model number and patent information. I was unable to find any picture of this clock in the catalogs that were available at the Bristol Museum or among the many of which I have copies.

      It is an interesting model, as there are two sides to the case, as well as an arched metal top. In finishing this clock, we decided to use a coppery bronze finish, which we felt might be quite similar to Japanese bronze, a color used in later offerings. It is a very appealing clock, featuring a large cherub resting among grape leaves.

      We will have to add this clock to the list of those without records – but signed, those without numbers or names and those without anything. Some day, I hope, someone will find records left behind by the Mullers. Then, maybe, it will be time for another chapter or book concerned with the life and business records of this notable firm.

Cherub and Grapes

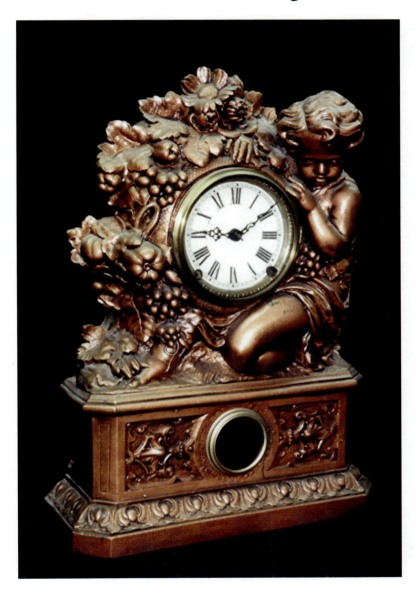

DOLPHIN

Number	61
Height:	20"
Movement:	8 day time & strike
Patent:	A. P.
Catalogs:	1858 – 1876
Prices:	8 day comp. bronze $8.75
	8 day Iron bronze $6.75

A dolphin is defined as any one of two widespread families (platanistidae and delphinidae) of toothed whales having high levels of intelligence and usually a beaklike snout.

This one piece (with attachments), two bezel case shows two dolphins located on either side of the top of a column. A classical figure of a woman and a child holding a harp appear at the top. There is a frieze at the base surrounding the bottom bezel.

This clock is fitted with a Nicholas Müller & Sons eight day time & strike movement. The implication is that this design was offered directly to the public exclusively, with their own movement and assembly. It has been implied that the sons purchased unmarked movements from others and stamped their name thereon. However, since all of this is speculation, they may actually have produced their own movements, thus increasing revenue for the firm.

Dolphin

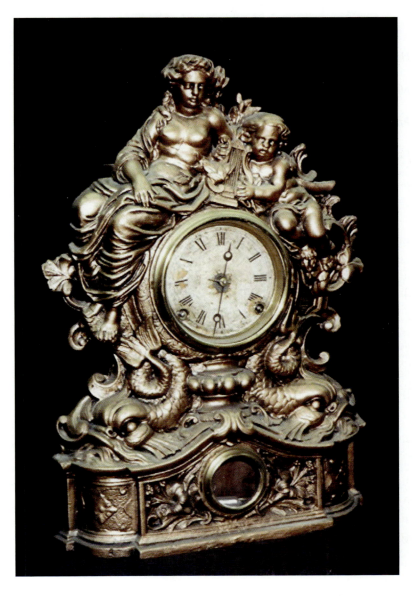

DOLPHIN

(Clock Stand)

Number:	600
Height:	20"
Movement:	Round alarm clock
Patent:	A. P.

When we first acquired this clock, is seemed that it was a blatant attempt to circumvent the patent on the case, by changing the bottom, to close up the pendulum bob opening and thus make it "different". It was also made of iron, which everyone assumed guaranteed it to be a fraud.

Once I was able to find several authoritative sources showing the manufacture of "Iron Bronze" clocks as well as "Composition bronze" of the same casting, it then became obvious that Müller offered "choices", offering some inexpensive alternatives to his own innovation – "Composition Bronze".

When the company numbered various other items manufactured by them, they used the numbers above 299 – the 300's possibly being one category, the 400's another. In my Nicholas Müller's Sons catalog, the imitation marble clocks were still using numbers in the mid 200's. This "clock stand" seems to have been the start of the 600's series.

Dolphin

SHEPHERD CHILDREN

Number:	62
Height:	17 ½"
Movement:	8 day time & strike and 30 hour same sized case
Patent:	1857
Catalogs:	1858 – 1876
Prices:	$5.00 - $8.25

Two children are beautifully shown on this casting, one wearing a straw hat and classical drapery, seen supporting the top bezel. The second child, hatless, sits just below and to the side of the bezel.

We have seen several examples of this model on which the conch shell, original to the design, is missing. This would significantly lower the value of the clock. Reeds and cattails grace the top of the case, with elephant ear foliage overall. More shells decorate the casting and flowers add to the decorative charm of the lower support.

Examples of this model have been found using movements by Seth Thomas, N. Pomeroy (ours) as well as The American Clock Co.

According to the price lists we have seen, the 8 day comp. bronze sold for $8.25, and the iron bronze 30 hour sold for $6.25. In another catalog, the prices were $7.00 for the comp. bronze eight day model and $5.00 for the 30 hour Iron Bronze. Once again, the difference in price between the Composition bronze and the Iron bronze were significant in both lists. It would seem that the cheaper models were doing well and continued to be offered.

Shepherd Children

RENAISSANCE

Number:	64
Height:	16"
Movement:	30 hour time & strike
Patent:	1858
Catalogs:	1865 – 1876
Price:	1874 - $6.00

The Renaissance is defined as a rebirth, the great revival of art, literature and learning in Europe in the 14th, 15th and 16th centuries, based on classical sources. It began in Italy and spread gradually to other countries and marked the transition from the medieval world to the modern. It was a rebirth of all the arts and sciences.

Here you will see another one piece front embellished with fruits and foliage as well as plenty of lush vegetation and the lush acanthus leaves. This is a true Renaissance design.

Renaissance

FOX AND HARE

Number:	65
Height:	19 ¾"
Movement:	8 day time & strike
Patent:	1856
Catalogs:	1858 – 1875
Prices:	Composition Bronze - $9.50 Iron Bronze - $7.75

    A Waterbury movement powers this example, although others may be found to have been used. As may be seen, our case is painted, very professionally, in natural colors. Most of the naturally painted examples that we have seen have been garishly painted, with primary colors standing out and spoiling the workmanship. Very realistic branches or roots can be seen, tastefully colored. A baby rabbit and a squirrel may be seen at the top, as well as lush foliage.

    In Aesop's Fables, many different stories were written about the fox and the hare. At times, the fox won the day and at other times the hare was the clear victor. This case shows that they both have eventually lost, since they appear to be deceased. Aesop wrote to illustrate the folly of risking too much – not thinking ahead. The trussed up animals tell a story as well as being a decorative part of this rustic scene. The intertwining roots are quite attractive.

Fox and Hare

SCOTCHMAN

Number:	66
Height:	18"
Movement:	8 day time & strike
Patent:	1858
Catalogs:	1858 – 1876
Prices:	Composition bronze – 8 day - $8.25
	Iron Bronze - $6.75

A man in the national garb of Scotland reclines on the lower bezel of this one-piece, two bezel front. His dog is at his side. Perhaps he is exhausted from hunting. He wears a "Tam-O-Shanter" (hat), as well as his kilt. The case is lush with vegetation.

The name Scotchman is a variation of "Scotsman" (the preferred form) and is defined as a native or inhabitant of Scotland – especially a man.

Movements found in several cases are both from the American Clock Co. and E. N. Welch.

Scotchman

HIGHLANDER

Number:	None
Height:	19 ½"
Movement:	8 day time & strike
Catalogs:	1865 – 1876
Patent:	1865
Prices:	1866 – 8 day t & s - comp. bronze - $8.25
	8 day T & S - Iron bronze - $6.50

    This is a superbly designed and executed one piece front with two bezels. Much superior craftsmanship is shown throughout the design, as compared with the Scotchman. This case was patented seven years after the Scotchman, but is not listed in any catalog with a number assigned to it, nor am I aware of any example having been found with a number. Perhaps it was a special order or commission and the distributor preferred the exclusivity.

    A Highlander is defined as a native or inhabitant of a mountainous region occupying nearly the entire Northern half of Scotland. The Second definition describes him as a soldier of a Highlands Regiment. Every bit of clothing, vegetation and even the dog are authentic to the region.

    The jaunty feather protruding from the tam is not a strong element but is an important one which could have easily broken off in handling. Fortunately, this vital artistic detail is intact on our "Highlander".

Highlander

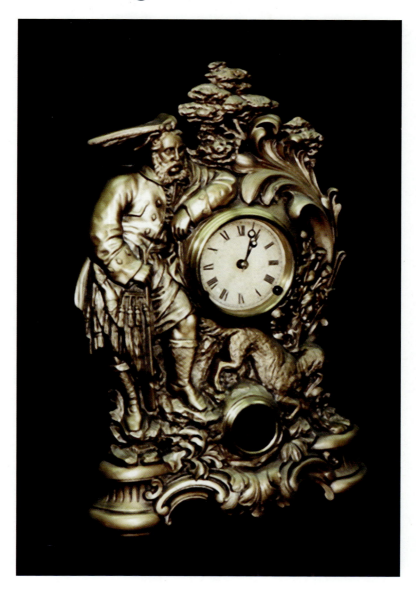

PEASANT GIRL

Number:	67
Height:	19"
Movement:	8 day time & strike
Patent::	1858
Catalogs:	1858 - 1875
Prices	$6.50 to $8.75

A lovely peasant girl in a large straw hat graces the top of the case – a one piece, two bezel model. The rabbits may be seen opposite her feet, above the pendulum bezel. Grapes and acanthus leaves decorate the entire clock.

As agriculture was extremely necessary in this growing country, as it is even today, it must have been a good seller. Careful marketing was essential to a business such as this.

In 1866, according to the price lists I have, the composition bronze clocks sold for $8.75. In 1877, however, the cost was lower - $8.25 - for the composition bronze and the Iron bronze, not listed before, was $6.50.

Peasant Girl

BEGGAR

Number:	69
Height:	17"
Movement:	8 day time & strike
Catalogs:	1872 – 1876
Patent:	A. P.
Price:	1875 - $8.75 – composition bronze

    We have a new generation of Müller clocks. Although they are still manufacturing one piece fronts, the newer models are now shorter one bezel decorative bases with tops, which are a complete unit, replacing the wooden tops used on the one piece fronts.

    A charming young lad rests atop the clock. He holds a walking stick and rests near a fence, which we have observed to be missing in several other clocks of this model. It would appear that there was poverty in this land of great promise, or perhaps it was a reminder of the harsh times that the immigrants endured prior to coming to America. In either case, the whole casting has great appeal.

Beggar

FISHER BOY

Number:	70
Height:	22 ½"
Movement:	8 day time & strike
Catalogs:	1872 – 1876
Price:	1874 & 75 - $16.75

    This case is an alternative model to # 93 – "Fisher Boy and Dog". It is more imposing, vertical and features a figural montage that is more pleasing to the eye. The boy is more dominant and handsome and the string of fish in this model is attached to the figure, which eliminates the possibility of loss.

    The base becomes a showcase to the top in this casting. The former model seems to minimize the importance of the figural grouping. As far as the merchandising appeal, a boy fishing would seem to be very desirable.

    This reminds me of my son's first fishing trip. He was thrilled when he landed his first little catch, but happiness turned to dismay when he ran to us screaming, "Ernie is going to kill my fish". All was well when the fish was released and my son's new hobby was short lived.

Fisher Boy

INNOCENCE

Number:	71A
Height:	11"
Movement:	1 day Terry Lever – time or time & strike
Catalogs:	1874 – 1876
Patent:	1874
Prices:	1875 - $7.00 - $7.50

One of five miniature Müller clocks that we have been able to purchase, "Innocence" is a small desirable clock due to the special Terry movement. It shows a young girl holding a lamb and is a companion representation with "Boy and Dog".

In Müller's numbering system, any number followed by a letter indicates that the clock is available with more than one complete top. The bases were the same in this model as well as "Boy and Dog", which has its own number (#82). These clocks were extremely popular at that time, as well as today. After all, combining children with the petite size of the clocks is always charming, but adding the collectability of Terry special lever movement makes this series a sure winner.

We have had several examples of model # 82 and have noticed that there can be a difference in size of the finished product of as much as ½" among the clocks. Chris Bailey states, "Some fronts came in two distinct sizes. Often a one day clock was smaller than the 8 day counterpart. In some instances the two close sizes, usually a half inch less difference, were given in various catalogs for a model, in which case we believe the fronts were the same but just measured differently. When two close sizes are given, the size given most frequently is underlined".

Innocence

CHASE AND PANTHEON

Number: 74

Size: 14 ½" (also made 22")

Movement: 8 day time & strike

Catalog: 1858

This clock is signed on the arched metal top. The label inside reads:

Manufactured & sold by American Clock Co.

Depot #3 Cortlandt Street, New York

The case has a metal front with one bezel, two metal sides and an arched metal top. It is quite different from previous Müller Company clocks. The front is the only decorated component, with an eagle above the dial. It has a stepped back base with a satyr holding a rope and tassel. The case is also decorated with the traditional acanthus leaves used in classical sculpture.

Beneath the dial are typical American themes such as The Articles of War, cotton bale, caduceus (medicine) and a lighthouse. The significance of the name has thus far eluded me. It is shown in several catalogs and the photograph shown here corresponds to the sketch in the catalogs.

Chase and Pantheon

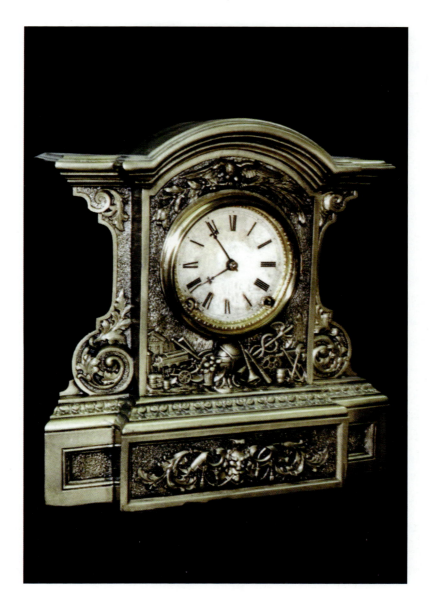

GARLAND

Number: 75

Height: 14 ½"

Movement: 8 day time & strike

Catalog: 1858

Patent:

The name of the casting is self-evident, as a lovely garland of flowers is strung beneath the single bezel on the clock. My husband recast this several times and used it to replace a missing component on a clock we would be offering for sale. As always, we kept the most perfect example of each model.

The clock is a rather plain but graceful model which we have left in its base metal, with a protective coating. Let me reiterate – Müller never sold his castings un-plated. We have done this because we wanted a contrast here and there to the large number that are finished in a similar fashion. If we only owned a few examples of Müller's work, we would surely want them to be finished in the most appropriate manner.

We have seen this model with movements by The American Clock Mfg. as well as Owen & Clark.

It is very plain for the period but seems to herald the Eastlake period of Victoriana. Eastlake was designing the "modern" of the Victorian style. It featured incised, rather than raised decorations, as may be seen below the pan.

Garland

LOUIS XV

Number:	77
Height:	18"
Movement:	8 day time & strike
Catalogs:	1858 – 1876
Patent:	
Price:	1874 - $14.50

When considering the name given to this casting, I felt that it was incongruous. The case, I felt, should be regal and possibly extravagant in its design. It is absolutely appropriately named, as you shall see.

Louis XIV was King of France from 1643-1715. His reign encompassed a period of flourishing French culture. Upon his death, he was succeeded by Louis XV, who ascended the throne at five years of age. He was the great-grandson of Louis XIV and was commonly called "The Boy King".

When we examine the case, we see a depiction of a young boy at play. A ball is close by. He reigned from 1715 – 1774, the date of his demise. He was succeeded by his grandson, Louis XVI (1754-1793) as King of France from 1774-1792. His reign was marked by the French Revolution and he died by the guillotine.

Louis XV

SETTER

Number:	79
Height:	16 ½"
Movement:	8 day time and strike
Catalogs:	1858 – 1875
Patent	
Prices:	1875 – composition bronze - $15.75

    The clock seen here consists of two major components – the beautifully executed hunting dog in repose and a rather elaborate, imposing base. Our example, as shown here, has an alarm dial at the center of the single bezel. The firm is always trying to keep up with competitors and to use the latest technology. There are two finials on either side of the dial pan and bezel.

    It is an attractively shaped case with some incised decorations. The top of the case is gently arched, giving the dog's resting place more emphasis.

    The dog is a universally revered animal and used as a representation of faithfulness and courage. Müller apparently recognized the popularity of the species and has made quite a few castings which feature the dog and his close relationship to humans. Among these are "Dog" #112B, "Boy and Dog" #82, "Fisher Boy and Dog" #93, "Indian Hunter" #181 (Chingachgook) and others. Once again Müller took into consideration the tastes and interests of the buying public.

Setter

MANTEL

Number:	81
Height:	7"
Movement:	Terry lever movement 1 day time & strike
Catalogs:	1865 – 1876
Patent:	1872
Price:	1874 - $4.75

This one of the smallest cases made by the firm and was called "Bronze" in an 1858 catalog. It is more architectural in design than earlier models and has a great deal of incised decoration and simple patterning, as contrasted with the sculptural cases in his earlier years. Perhaps some of the design responsibilities were being assumed by his sons (Herman, in particular).

It is also true that Victorian furniture was shifting from the ornate and Rococo of earlier Victoriana. Victoria was the longest reigning English monarch, her reign having spanned more than 60 years and the styles of Victoriana range from the Rococo to the fringe of Art Deco. Other monarchs, such as Napoleon, had only twenty years of furniture attributed to their tenure (Empire style). Müller, once again, seemed to constantly keep abreast of trends and furniture styles and has a great aptitude for merchandising.

I passed this clock several times at a Mart because of its simplicity and size, neither of which were consistent with his other work.

Mantel

BOY AND DOG

Number:	82
Height:	11"
Movement:	Terry lever – one day time and 1 day T & S
Catalogs:	1867 – 1876
Patent:	1872
Prices:	1874 - $7.00 time only - $7.50 t & s

"Boy and Dog" has achieved higher auction prices than most other castings. There may be many reasons – the theme is universally popular – and the Terry movement has many advocates. This is a beautifully conceived and executed example of Müller's skill. There are also people who admire the compact size.

This is a very adaptable clock. It does not merely serve as a mantel decoration, but may be used throughout the house – desktop, bedroom, end table, etc. The clock is very sculptural in all aspects and is very pleasing to the eye.

It shares the same base as "Innocence" and is often sought after as a pair – boy & dog – girl & lamb.

Boy and Dog

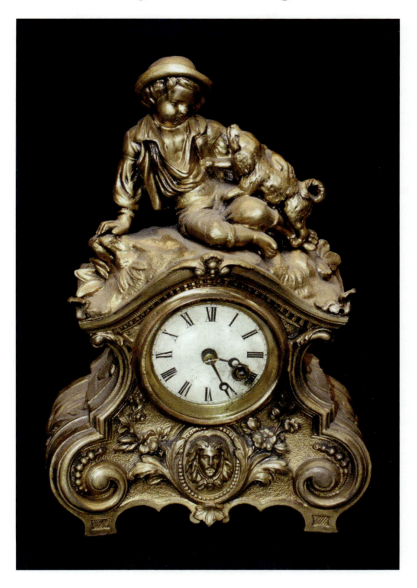

TROUBADOUR

Number: Unknown

Height: 19"

Catalog:

Patent:

    A charming medieval case shows a man playing a stringed instrument, a church window, vegetation and scenes of an old town. By definition, "a troubadour is any of a class of lyric poets and poet musicians in Southern France and Northern Spain and Italy during the 11th through 13th century, who wrote poems and songs of love and chivalry, usually with intricate stanza form and rhyme scheme".

    Although there are no identifying markings on the case, I was able to find it pictured in an old catalog in the Bristol Museum. Unfortunately, I failed to make note of the catalog and years, but I intend to do just that on my next visit. We sent the casting to Texas 30 years ago and Jim Shawn agreed that it was characteristic of Müller's work in every way. My "gut instincts" realized the truth long before the proof was found.

Troubadour

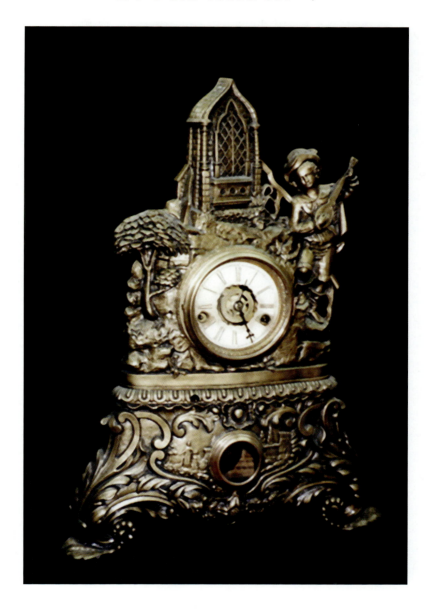

GLOBE

Number :	84
Height:	20"
Movement:	8 day time & strike
Catalogs:	1858 – 1867
Patent:	A. P.
Prices:	1866 - $8.25

    Having been a teacher for so many years, I believe that this clock portrays all aspects of education. On this large one piece front are shown two classically garbed children on either side of the top bezel. Within the elements of this case may be found a globe, centered below the top bezel, a harp (music), an oval picture in a frame (art), books (literature), plants (nature), birds (nature) and an inkwell & pen (writing).

    It took me many years to find but I consider it to be a personal favorite. The "divi divi" trees lend a graceful look to the top section of the clock. We have seen this clock with both Waterbury Clock Co. and Seth Thomas movements.

    From time to time, I meet my former students or their parents and somehow I can picture their faces even after 50 years. It happened last week, once again, and I asked an unfamiliar woman whether she had a daughter named "Marianne". She did and also remembered me and told me how I had changed her daughter's life. I have a little box inscribed, "Teaching changes lives" – it does - both theirs and mine.

Globe

DOVE

Number:	85
Height:	9"
Movement:	Terry lever – one day time & 1 day time & strike
Catalogs:	1865 – 1876
Patent:	
Prices:	1874 - $4.50 – 1 day time - $5.00 1 day t&s

    This is another example that almost escaped me. The diminutive size, as well as the lack of familiar ornamentation, detail and dimension, seemed less likely to be a Müller product. It is also less attractive and well executed than other Mullers, in my opinion.

    The bird at the top is not as well defined as are the grapes and foliage. It is clearly marked and its differences make it a welcome part of any Müller collection.

    Few symbols have a tradition as long and rich as the dove. It is a particular favorite in art and iconography. Doves are symbols of love, peace, innocence, gentleness, faith, marital affection and constancy.

    Doves often represent the divine. The Christian dove represents the Holy Spirit or Holy Ghost. Doves appear in the symbology of Judaism, as well.

Dove

PATCHEN

Number:	88
Height:	21 ½"
Movement:	8 day time & strike
Catalogs:	1865 – 1876
Patent:	1882
Prices:	1884 - $15.75

The famous trotting horse, George M. Patchen Jr., "Champion of the Turf" is immortalized on this clock, which is composed of two major pieces. Trotting was the primary form of horse racing at this time in history and this horse enjoyed the same type of fame as Man O' War in later years.

Patchen was the property of Wm. Louis Maurer (1860). His attributes have been described as follows: "The high stepping action of the Morgan breed and the medium gait of the Clay line, including Patchen, combined with the long stride of Messinger to produce the swift front stroke found in today's trotter".

Currier & Ives created a beautiful lithograph, colored by hand – sheet size 24 7/8" x 32 ½", of Trotting Stallion George M. Patchen – a dramatic view of the New Jersey bred stallion at full stretch, 1857.

Our model (shown) is powered by a movement marked "Nicholas Müller & Sons".

Patchen

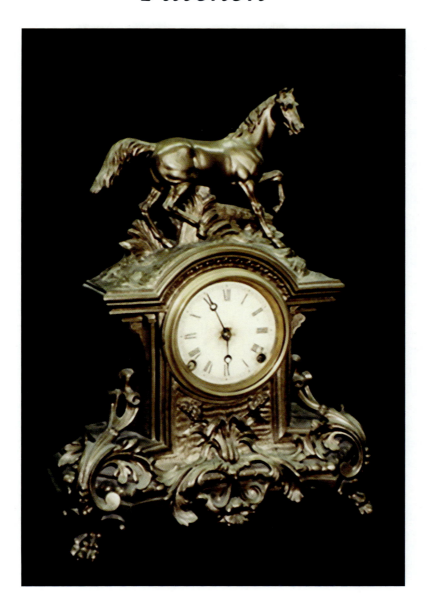

FISHER BOY AND DOG

(New style)

Number:	93
Height:	22 ½"
Movement:	8 day time & strike
Catalogs:	1874 – 1876
Patent:	A. P.
Price:	1874 - $16.75

The base on this casting is the same as the one used for "Goat" #99. It is used with different tops and different numbers, unlike previous use of the same base with a choice of tops using the same number and differentiating with a succession of letters identifying the tops.

This model is beautifully designed and artistically conceived. The entire clock is reminiscent of his earlier works. It has been found containing Seth Thomas and Florence Kroeber movements.

A boy stands by a tree stump – holding a string of fish. The fish are often missing from the case, since they are hanging from a wire and may have been easily broken off and lost. A tackle box is at his feet.

Fisher Boy and Dog

BOY HOLDING TORCH

Number: 93?

Height: 16"

Movement: 8 day time & strike

The base of this casting is identical with that of "Fisher Boy and Dog".

These tops are interchangeable. The decorative components appear to be consistent with Müller's work. The male figure atop the clock is Scottish in design and the entire case appears to have been brass plated. This was obviously the owner's choice of finish and is dissimilar from most of the work done by the firm. I do recall seeing an article offering a later list of finishes available from the company. It was mentioned that a particular brass was offered but do feel that this is not a characteristic finish on these clocks.

Years before we found #93, we suspected that this "Boy Holding Torch" (my appellation) was indeed a Müller product. I sent it to Mr. Shawn for his opinion and found him to be in agreement. Comparing the two cases, it became obvious that our initial identification was correct.

Boy Holding Torch

SAILOR

Number:	95
Height:	17 ½"
Movement:	8 day time & strike
Catalogs:	1869 – 1876
Patent:	A. P.
Prices:	1874 - $11.25

"Sailor" is a one piece, one bezel front with many additions. Our example houses an E. N. Welch movement. After seeing this casting in an old reprinted catalog, it went to Number One on my "Most Wanted List". I finally spied it in the back of an old garage in Brooklyn. It had taken 25 years to actually obtain, but was worth the effort.

It is a beautifully executed case representing all things nautical. A mariner wearing the old style boater's hat dominates the design of the case. The nautical accoutrements include ropes, chains and an anchor depicted artistically around the bezel.

Having been surrounded by clocks made by Müller for over 35 years, it is my strong feeling that this dramatically designed casting would have had to be designed by either Nicholas, himself, or by his brother Karl. I am still looking for "The Miner", which strongly reminds me of the "Sailor" and was certainly designed by the same hand. You will find the patent application picture of the "Miner" in the Patent Chapter., later in this volume. You will see that the patent for "Miner" was filed by Karl Müller on August 31st, 1869.

Karl Müller was the eminent sculptor of his time in Europe and Nicholas was listed as a worker involved in the casting of his brother's designs. There is strong evidence that Karl left behind many designs that were later patented in his name by his brother Nicholas' firm.

Sailor

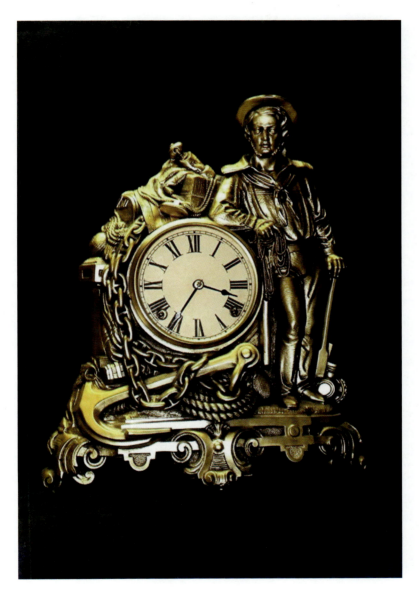

GOAT

Number: 99

Height: 18"

Movement: 8 day time & strike

Patent:

Prices: 1875 - $14.00

    This handsome case was designed during Nicholas Müller's lifetime and is a representation of his exquisite attention to details. Once again, this might have been a casting designed by his brother, Karl. We have been unable to find a copy of the patent, if any, filed by the firm. Judging from the sculptural expertise, at its best in this model, it was done by the hand of a master. The "Goat" top may have been the design of Karl and the base that of his brother.

    The identical base for this # 99 model was also used on case # 93, "Fisher Boy and Dog". The two are only six numbers apart, yet they have two distinctly different numbers in his numerical sequence. Perhaps the former practice that used the same number for the base and an additional letter for each different top was confusing and therefore discarded. Looking closely at both tops, it is my feeling that they were done by different hands.

    This case would have additional appeal to agriculturalists as well animal lovers.

Goat

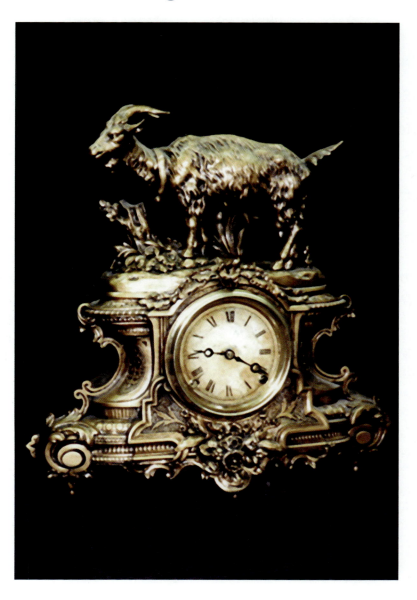

ESMERELDA

Number:	none
Height:	18"
Movement:	8 day time & strike
Patent:	
Price:	1874 - $11.75

The main figure in the casting is a representation of a girl in a French literary classic, "Notre Dame de Paris / The Hunchback of Notre Dame" (1836) by Victor Hugo.

La Esmerelda, the lost daughter of Sister Gudule, is a beautiful gypsy street dancer. Along with her goat, Djali, she charms everyone with her stunning looks and magic tricks. She keeps an amulet and other trinkets around her neck to help her find her parents. Her goat is her constant companion.

The case consists of two major pieces and is beautifully sculpted, obviously the work of Karl or Nicholas. It is once again possible that Karl, the master sculptor, designed the top and Nicholas the bottom. Check this model for any missing parts, as we have seen this without the goat, which is so crucial to the theme of the clock.

Esmerelda

REAPER

Number:	101
Size:	18 ½"
Movement:	8 day time & strike
Catalogs:	1865 – 1880
Patent:	A. P.
Prices:	1874 - $14.00

By definition, a Reaper is someone who "gathers harvest or crop by cutting", which is usually done with a scythe, sickle or reaping machine. In the casting, the girl doing the reaping may be clearly seen tying up a sheaf of wheat, which is part of the process of gathering the crop.

This case is once again two deliberate parts – the decorative base and the statuary laden top. The base is rather generic and could be used in several different themes. This clock has a Waterbury Clock Co. movement.

Please continue on the next two pages which give a marvelous new aspect to this otherwise typical case.

Reaper

MATTHEW BRADY'S CLOCK

An article entitled "Matthew Brady's Clock" appeared in the NAWCC Bulletin, October 2002, Volume 44/5, No. 340, authored by Bob Frishman, an NAWCC member from Andover, Massachusetts. In a meticulously researched and fascinating account, he tells of examining more than 7,000 portraits taken by Brady, finding more than 60 images that included the clock Müller named "The Reaper".

Many important people were represented within this group. Among those pictured with the clock were General George Custer, Clara Barton and Robert E. Lee. Mr. Frishman has graciously allowed me to include some of those photographs. The clock seems to have been one of the "props" used in Brady's portraits.

It is interesting to speculate on just how this clock might have come into Brady's possession. Suppose we compare the biographical information that we already have about Nicholas Müller with the information provided by Mr. Frishman in his article.

Nicholas Müller and Matthew Brady were contemporaries, Müller having been born in 1818 and Brady in 1823 – just five years apart. Brady started business in New York City in 1844, Müller in 1849 – same city – just five years apart. Brady went bankrupt in 1873 (the same year that Muller died). Brady died virtually penniless in 1896 (the last year that Herman Müller, Nicholas' son, was involved in the firm Nicholas Müller's Sons & Company).

Both men led parallel and overlapping lives. Both achieved considerable measures of fame at the same time and in the same place. Both worked within the artistic community and were prolific in their endeavors.

It is not out of the realm of possibility that they were acquainted and that Brady may have acquired "The Reaper" either by purchase or as a gift from a friend, possibly Nicholas Müller.

Robert E. Lee

Clara Barton

General David Hunter and others

ALHAMBRA

Number:	104
Height:	14"
Movement:	8 day time & strike
Catalogs:	1869 – 1876
Patent:	1868
Prices:	1874 - $11.25

"During the 19th century, "The Grand Tour of Europe" was considered by the aristocracy of Europe, as well as wealthy Americans to be a necessary part of growing up", according to Sir Edward Bulwer – The Last Days of Pompeii – 1934.

New Yorker Washington Irving wrote "Tales of the Alhambra" in 1829. It was published in 1832 and gave insights into its architecture and culture, as well as Moorish legends associated with it.

The Alhambra is a walled city and fortress in Grenada, Spain. It was built from 1238 – 1492 and is lavishly decorated overall. Islamic Art does not use representations of living things, but heavily relies on geometric patterns, especially symmetric (repeating patterns). We were fortunate to have visited The Alhambra some years ago and brought back a large book containing color photos of the decorations. Upon examination, Müller's interpretation was very well executed.

This casting is Müller's interpretation of the decorative elements of the Alhambra, which is not only the most beautiful but the oldest and best preserved of the ancient Arab palaces or rather, it is the only one still in existence.

Alhambra

GUARDIAN

Number:	107
Height:	17"
Movement:	8 day time & strike
Catalog:	1967 – 1876
Patent:	A. P.
Price:	1874 - $11.00

"Guardian" is an emotionally pleasing model, more reminiscent of the ornate earlier cases. This one, patented after the death of Nicholas in March of 1873, was his work as well, since it was shown and offered for sale in catalogs prior to his death. It appears that some patents seem to have been granted many years after the initial patent application. There could be many reasons for these delays.

According to Stacy Wood, Nicholas held more than 40 patents for case fronts in that brief 20 year period, as well as a far greater number for which he did not seek patent rights.

As the title suggests, the dog is guarding the sleeping boy – protecting him. This clock was available with two different dials – one, a Tucker Bronze cast metal dial (black), as well as one made with white porcelain. The example pictured has an N. Pomeroy movement.

Guardian

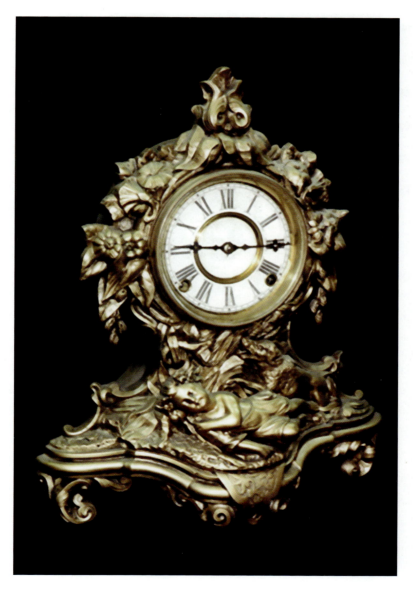

EVANGELINE

Number:	108A
Height:	17"
Movement:	8 day time & strike
Catalogs:	1865 – 1880
Patent:	1874
Price:	1874 - $9.75

    Henry Wadsworth Longfellow's first epic poem, "Evangeline: A Tale of Acadie" was published in 1847. The poem elevated Longfellow to be the most famous writer in America. Müller capitalized on this recent publication and made a case commemorating the new heroine.

    This book is one of the best illustrations of faithfulness and the constancy of woman. "Evangeline never wavered in her quest to find her lost love, from whom she was separated on their wedding day by the British expulsion of the French speaking inhabitants of Nova Scotia", according to Longfellow.

    This top is used on the same base as "Bird's Nest" #108B and "Vintner" # 108V. I would assume that the "B" is for bird and the "V" is for Vintner. This example is powered by an E.N. Welch movement.

Evangeline

BIRD'S NEST

Number:	108B
Height:	19"
Movement:	8 day time & strike
Catalogs:	1874 – 1876
Patent:	1874
Price:	1874 - $9.75

    The customer had a choice of at least three different tops, (each named to describe the central figure). Most people, I feel, would have looked at the whole clock and chosen the one they liked. Unless there was a particular base that they preferred, they might have been unaware of the duplication of bases. The names were different, after all.

    The tops are made to interchange with just a few screws, making it possible to choose a vignette most pleasing to the purchaser. It also reduces the number of bases that must be manufactured by allowing one base to easily become three clocks. The dials on these three models differ as well, suggesting that different movement manufacturers used their own choices of dials.

    This model illustrates a woman leaning over to view a bird's nest in a wooded area. It is the only Müller clock we have ever auctioned. We chose one of the top three auction houses in New York City for our little "test run". The price obtained was three times our estimated figure due, we were told, to the fact that Müller had inscribed his name, number (and the fact that it was made in New York) in plain view on the top piece, next to the nest. All antiques attain their highest prices in the country of origin. Hence, a New York clock will bring the greatest return in New York.

Bird's Nest

VINTNER

Number:	108 V
Height:	19"
Movement:	8 day time & strike
Catalog:	1865 – 1876
Patent:	1874
Price:	1874 – 1875 - $9.75

Once again, this clock uses a base that may be fitted with a choice of at least three tops. The two other tops we show are "Evangeline" and "Bird's Nest". This top depicts a man with a basket of grapes, used in winemaking.

A vintner, by definition, is a person who makes wine, being a fermented juice of grapes, used as an alcoholic beverage as well as in cooking. The designer of this clock is seeking a marketplace for the various clocks manufactured by the company. For thousands of years grapes have been used in the wine making process and wine has been a very important consumable liquid. The "Vintner" most likely was a very desirable casting.

Vintner

ARMORER

Number:	109
Height:	17 ¾"
Movement:	8 day time & strike
Catalogs:	1865 – 1876
Patent:	A. P.
Price:	1874 – 5 - $13.50

    This case, quite a handsome two piece example, decorated with vines and ivy leaves, depicts a putti (or cherub) making armor. He is shown beating iron with a hammer against an anvil. Historically, an armorer is defined as "a person who made or repaired armor and arms". It is important that the hammer is present in this piece, or the value will be significantly reduced.

    The vines are artistically arranged and compliment the overall aesthetics of the case. A one bezel, two major parts model, this one has a Seth Thomas movement. The graceful overall nature of the design makes this a personal favorite.

Armorer

FALCON

Number:	unknown
Height:	16"
Movement:	8 day time & strike
Catalogs:	1874
Patent:	
Price:	

    Falcon is another un-numbered case. This lack of identification may have been the preference of the movement maker or distributor and could have been solely available in that name.

    Looking at this clock, we see a falconer (one who hunts with falcons) holding a bird which projects out in a three-dimensional effect.

    A falcon is defined as any bird of prey trained to hunt and kill small game. In falconry, the female is called a falcon and the male a Tiercel. These birds usually have long pointed wings and a short, curved, notched beak.

Falcon

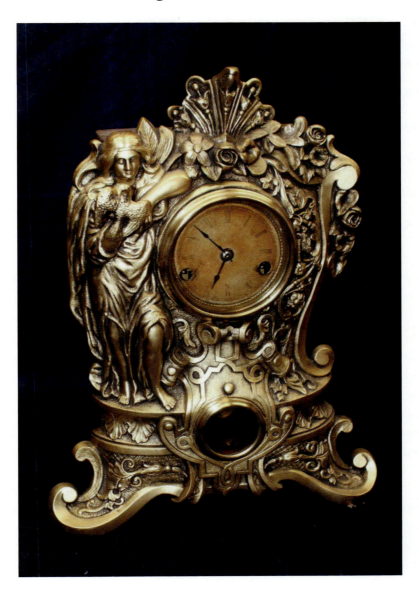

MOUNTAINEER

Number:	110
Height:	20"
Movement:	8 day time & strike
Catalogs:	1865 – 1876
Patent:	A. P.
Price:	1874 - $14.00

    We initially found this model painted in "natural colors, (my term). It was quite colorful and, when we found another with a bronze-like finish, we were able to sell it quite easily. In your refinishing, you have choices. Art, after all, is "truly in the eyes of the beholder". It is important for the boy to have his walking stick. When we first acquired the painted model, the stick was missing. We assumed that he should have had a rifle, so I purchased a model sized replica of a rifle. We thought it was appropriate until we found the second clock, having its original walking stick. George was then able to copy the original and replace the gun. Had we been able to check the catalogs that we later obtained, we would have seen the actual size and scale of the missing piece.

    A mountaineer is defined as a person who lives in a mountainous region; a mountain climber. Both clocks had Seth Thomas movements. It was also marketed with a flat top – no figural grouping – and was called "Swan", for obvious reasons, stood 13" high and bore the same number #110 as the mountaineer. This appears to be another deviation in Müller's numerical system.

Mountaineer

AMOR

(OR AMOUR)

Number:	111
Height:	19 ¾"
Movement:	8 day time & strike
Catalogs:	1865 1876
Patent:	A. P.
Price:	1874 - $19.50

Truly a clock for lovers, this charming casting shows Cupid with his traditional bow and arrow, depicting love resulting from a meeting with cupid's arrow. The Roman myth tells of the God of Love, son of Venus, usually represented as a winged boy with bow and arrow and is identified with the Greek Eros.

It is interesting to see the steady rise in the cost of Müller's clocks over the last fifteen years. We could speculate that his product became more popular, hence "supply and demand", or it could indicate that the overall economy was steadily improving and prices rose as a result.

The finish used on this clock, as well as some of the others, was a "Plater's Spray' which was very shortly discontinued. It was a perfect finish and came in several very beautiful shades. No doubt there is something available now that would replicate a true bronze finish. Professional plating is another choice.

Amor or Amour

GLEANER

Number:	112
Height:	18 ¾"
Movement:	8 day time & strike
Catalogs:	1865 – 1876
Patent:	A. P.
Price:	1874 - $10.25

    A Gleaner is defined as one who collects the remaining grain from a reaped field. This case shows a woman with a scythe in her hand. It also shows or depicts a rabbit, which could suggest that animals, as well as humans, often subsist on the "leavings" after harvest.

    Two artistic elements combine to form this clock, a single bezel style. Similar festoons have been seen on earlier models.

    Both Waterbury and Kroeber movements have been found in this model.

    The "Gleaner" might be used as a companion piece to The "Reaper". Since they both deal with aspects of agriculture, they could make a nice grouping.

Gleaner

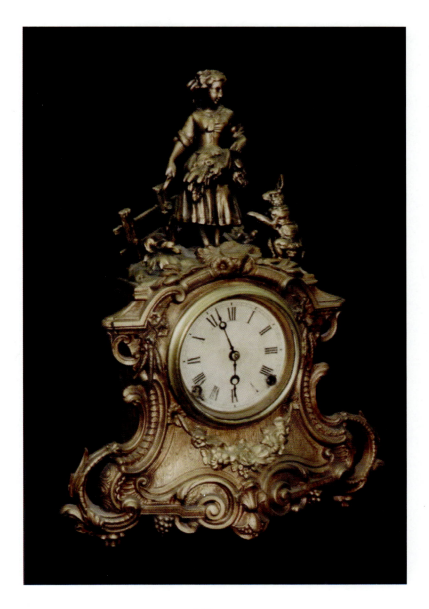

WINE DRINKER

Number:	116
Height:	20"
Movement:	8 day time & strike
Patent:	A. P.
Catalogs:	1867 – 1876
Price:	1874 - $15.75

This case shows a man adjacent to a cask of wine, seemingly enjoying his drink and celebrating. At first it seems incongruous that two children should be depicted below the bezel. On further examination, it appears that the heads are of different sizes, suggesting that a mother and child are removed from the celebrating. On the other hand, perhaps the mother is shielding or protecting the child from the father's excesses.

The case is gracefully ornamented with grapes and grape vines, which are appropriate when speaking of wine. This is an absolutely charming casting that has great appeal to this day.

Wine Drinker

ETRUSCAN NO. 1

Number:	118
Height:	19"
Movement:	8 day time & strike
Catalogs:	1867
Patent:	A. P.
Price:	1875 - $15.00

An Etruscan is a native of Etruria, an ancient 6th century area, occupying what is now Tuscany and part of Umbria in west central Italy. The Etruscans were the single most important influence on Roman culture in its transition to civilization. They were a sophisticated people, with original sculptural and painting tradition and an alphabet based on that of the Greeks. It was a dominant civilization.

This casting is one of three different models, listed as Etruscan 1, 2 and 3. Number 1, in my opinion, is the most attractive of the three, due to the fluidity of design, the graceful line to the legs and the intricacy of the handled urn on top. The lid of the urn lifts off, allowing for key storage. Some examples I have seen are missing their lids, which greatly affects their value.

This clock has a Waterbury 8 day movement. Three different dials were offered – Tucker bronze style cast metal and another with a white porcelain dial, as well as the traditional paper dial seen here.

Etruscan No.1

RUIN

Number:	120
Height:	13" – 18 ½"
Movement:	8 day time & strike
Catalogs:	1874 – 1876
Patent:	A. P.
Price:	1874 – 75 - $8.25

This casting depicts decay, showing rats, moths, slugs – all may be evident when a building falls into a state of decay or ruin. This clock has a movement made by Waterbury Clock Co.

We acquired a second example of "Ruin" shortly after the first, and offered it for sale. A woman was very interested in the clock but quickly turned away when she heard my enthusiastic narrative about the creatures pictured thereon. It sold quickly when I pointed out the positives.

On the next pages you will find what I consider to be the counterpart of "Ruin". It may have been created to precede or follow "Ruin".

Ruin

Counterpart to Ruin

Number: Unknown

Height: 14

Movement: 8 day time & strike

Patent:

      This would appear to be the counterpart to "Ruin", either preceding or following that model. The building and dimensions are the same, but it would seem to depict a renaissance – birds have built a nest and seem to be feeding fledglings. This is a healthy picture of the identical building at two stages of its life. Even the rodent appears less threatening. The brick work is the same but the atmosphere is positive. "Ruin" is a negative view of the same scene.

      This casting is made of iron. I haven't come across any iron castings for many years.

Counterpart to Ruin

CHASE AND FIGURE

Number :   122

Height: 20"

Movement: 8 day time & strike

Catalog: 1867

Patent: A. P.

Featured here is an ample amount of foliage above and beside the two bezels. Between the two bezels is pictured the chase – two dogs attacking a deer. This clock could have appealed to hunters.

At the base are incised designs, more characteristic of a later period. Perhaps this is an area that was worked by the sons. The details are not as crisp and precise.

As may be seen in its picture, it is a single front with two bezels. This configuration was characteristic of earlier Müller designs. Our clock contains a Waterbury Clock Co. movement.

Chase & Figure

AMAZON

Number:	unknown
Height:	16 ½"
Movement:	8 day time & strike
Patent:	
Catalogs:	1874 – 76
Price:	1874/5 - $19.50

    "Amazon" is one of a series of four different versions using the same base. These include "Savoyard", "Fanchon #2", "Mustang" and "Amazon". None of the four models are identified with numbers. Within Müller's numbering system, cases that have a variety of tops each bear the case number with an accompanying letter. (161 and 161A, e.g.). This system seems inconsistent in certain instances. I do feel, once again, that the clocks were probably shown totally assembled in each complete model. The customer could have been unaware of the repeated use of the bottom case unit. By showing the tops separately, it would have tended to confuse the potential buyer.

    The word "Amazon" could either have been referring to groups living in the Amazonian areas of South America or the legendary tribe of large powerful women. It is your choice to determine which definition better describes this case.

Amazon

SAVOYARD

Number:	unknown
Height:	18 ½"
Movement:	8 day time & strike
Catalogs:	1865 – 1876
Patent:	
Price:	1874 - $8.75

The base of this casting is numbered and signed. The top is also signed Müller. This clock appears to be a rather attractive "marriage". The top has been attached to the base in a very atypical manner. We bought it because it is a signed case but yet not "Müller". The craftsmanship of both pieces is there, but the blend of the two pieces is obviously not original.

The term Savoyard refers to a native or inhabitant of Savoy, a region in southeast France, on the borders of Italy and Switzerland, a former duchy and part of the kingdom of Sardinia, annexed by France in 1860.

"Savoyard" is shown in catalogs with a figure and animal. The top shown here was interestingly "married" but would not have the value of the original. Furthermore, the top and base appear to have been designed by different artists. The top is by far more professionally created and executed.

Savoyard

FANCHON No.2

Number:	unknown
Height:	18 ½"
Movement:	8 day time & strike
Catalogs:	1874 – 1876
Patent:	A. P.
Price:	1874 - $8.75

This is a charming two major piece clock showing a girl feeding birds. This example has a Waterbury movement.

Fanchon #2 was the second moralistic tale told in "Child Life in Town & Country" by Anatole France. In this story, Fanchon, a young girl, visited her grandmother's garden. She began eating her bread and soon dozens of birds surrounded her looking for food. She was too kindhearted to deny bread to all who paid for it with song.

She noticed that the birds differed. The aggressive ones left nothing for others. There is no fairness in this, she thought. All should have a turn, but this is not how the world works. She tried to help the weak and timid, but try as she would, the fat birds were fed at the expense of the thin ones.

It is interesting to speculate about the reason certain topics were chosen to be immortalized in these models. Were the Müllers very literate? Did they travel extensively before or after arriving in America? Were some cases commissioned? Perhaps records will be found to answer these questions.

Fanchon No. 2

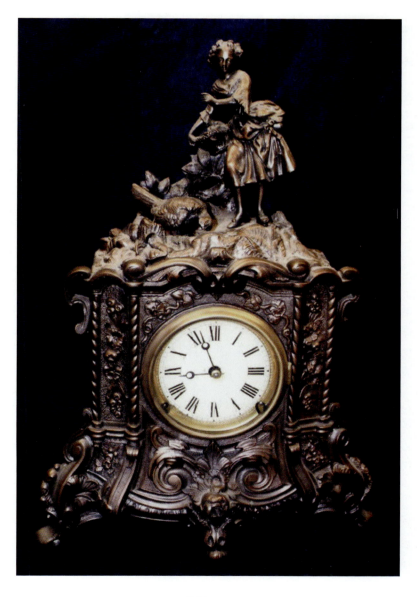

BALL PLAYERS

Number:	135
Height:	16"
Movement:	8 day time & strike – also 30 hour
Catalogs:	1869 - 1875
Patent:	A. P.- patented October 20, 1868
Prices:	1875 - $8.25 – 8 day
	1875 - $7.00 – 30 hour

An extremely elusive clock to find, this is one of the most sought-after models, due in part to the popularity of "The National Pastime". The case was designed and patented by Karl Müller and was first offered for sale in 1869. It was still offered in 1875 by the Waterbury Clock Co. of Waterbury, Connecticut.

A copy of the patent details and a fascinating NAWCC Journal article follow. The article was entitled "The Baseball Clock" and appeared in Volume 20, issue 196, on page 500. A few years ago this model attained four figures at auction.

Ball Players

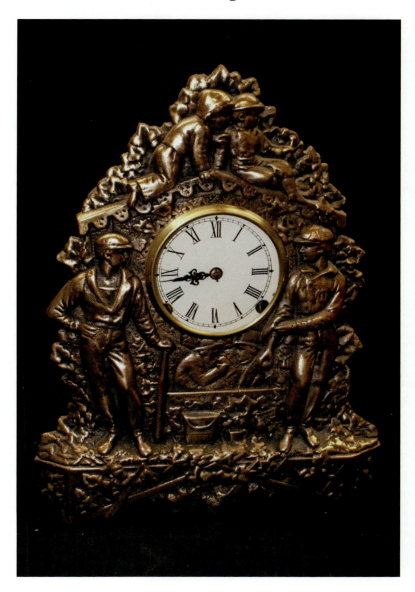

KARL MÜLLER, OF NEW YORK, N. Y., ASSIGNOR TO NICHOLAS MÜLLER, OF SAME PLACE.

Design No. 3,212, dated October 20, 1868.

DESIGN FOR A CLOCK-CASE.

The Schedule referred to in these Letters Patent and making part of the same.

To all whom it may concern:

Be it known that I, CARL MÜLLER, of the city, county, and State of New York, have invented a new and useful Design for a Clock-Case; and I do hereby declare that the following is a full, clear, and exact description thereof, which will enable those skilled in the art to make and use the same, reference being had to the accompanying photograph, forming a part of this specification, which photograph represents a front view of the design.

This invention relates to a design for a clock-case, representing the national game of base-ball.

For convenience in description, the design may be divided into two parts, $a\ a$ and $b\ b$, the latter representing the base or lower portion of the clock-case, while the former is the upper portion or case proper.

Two figures, representing the "pitcher" and "batter," one on each side of the case, form the main feature of the design. The pitcher is rolling up his right sleeve, and has a ball in his hand; the batter rests his left upon the bat, while his right lies on his hip. Both are clad in base-ball costume—caps, shirts, and pantaloons tied around the ankle.

Between the figures is the dial-hole, with a chain of ornaments, as seen in the photograph, around it, and above that a sharp roof-shaped top, on which two boys may be seen playing, one on his knees, and the other sitting, holding a bat in his hand.

In the background, under the dial-hole, and between the figures, two reporters are sitting, one with a book and pen in his hand. In front of and below them is a fence, to stop all stray balls.

In the foreground stands a water-pail, with a cup beside it.

The base of the design, $b\ b$, on which the two main figures rest, and which support the part $a\ a$, is formed by a series of bars and cross-bars, arranged as seen in the photograph.

The background, as well as the outline of the whole structure, is formed by ivy-leaves and branches entwined here and there.

What I claim as new, and desire to secure by Letters Patent, is—

The design for a clock-case, as herein shown and described.

The above specification signed by me, this 28th day of August, 1868.

KARL MÜLLER.

HENRY RASSIGA,
CHARLES KITSCHELT.

THE
BASEBALL
CLOCK

by
Mary Jane Strickler (PA)

Anyone for clocks and baseball? With the thought that we will not strike out altogether, this article is being offered for our clock-baseball buffs. This clock is *NOT* just a clock for it tells a story of the founders of America's number one sport.

By now you may be asking yourself (if you are so inclined to this practice): is this feminist throwing me a balk or trying to lead me afoul? Please be assured that this authoress has called upon a mere masculine-type to run the bases in researching this unique timepiece. It is with grateful appreciation that the following knowledge of Dan Ginsburg is shared.

The figures depicted in the cast iron front of this clock appear to be modelled after real people connected with the game of baseball. In comparing the pictures on their plaques in the Baseball Hall of Fame we discovered that the man in the background who is writing (to the left), is Henry Chadwick, and the man to his right in the top hat is Alexander Cartwright. Mr. Chadwick was the most famous sportswriter of the 19th century and the inventor of the box score. Mr. Cartwright revised primitive bat and ball games, such as townball, into baseball as we know it today, and is considered the inventor of baseball.

The ball players standing on either side of the dial are not so easily recognized. The man holding the ball is no doubt a pitcher for the New York Mutuals, who in their six-year history (1871-1876), had three men share this position. He is definitely not Candy Cummings, judging from the picture at hand. He is probably not Rynie Wolters, who only pitched for the Mutuals for one year (1871). Therefore, using the process of elimination, our man is probably the famous pitcher, Bobby Mathews, who appeared for the Mutuals from 1873 to 1876. Mr. Mathews has the distinction of pitching and winning the first major league game in history, back in 1871.

The only clue to the identification of the player leaning on the bat is the small insignia on the right side of his uniform which makes it appear as if he was a member of the Brooklyn Atlantics, making the game a local rivalry. Bob Ferguson was the manager and the best player on the team, so it might be him.

This clock carries a past, present, and future scene. Chadwick and Cartwright, the pioneers, are the past. The two players are the present. The children shown on the top of the dial represent the future of this perpetually great sport of baseball.

500

EGYPTIAN

Number:	138
Height:	10 ½"
Movement:	8 day time & strike
Catalogs:	1874 - 1876
Patent:	A. P.
Prices:	1875 - $6.00 - 8 day
	1875 - $4.75 - 30 hour

    This case is the most "modern" of the several cases offered with an Egyptian theme. There is a definite Eastlake look to this casting, and we are seeing a shift from the ornately carved to cleaner, plainer designs. Now that Nicholas has passed away, the boys were faced with establishing the skills and responsibilities that each of them was to assume.

    Why, I wondered, were there so many Egyptian themed clocks? I looked further. Although Egyptian influence on European history dates back more than 5,000 years, there wasn't too much interest in the country until, during the last half of the 19th century , steam and rail accessibility came to Egypt. Travelers brought back souvenirs – many of them going back 1,000 years. It was at this time that vast numbers of ancient artifacts were spirited out of the country. At this time Egypt's first museums were originated to save and protect antiquities.

    This period of time (which happened to co-inside with Müller's production years) was called The Egyptian Revival.

Egyptian

MINERVA

Number:	141
Height:	15" – 13" – 30 hour
Movement:	8 day time & strike and 30 hour
Catalogs:	1872 - 1876
Patent:	A. P.
Prices:	1874 - $6.00 - one day
	1874 - $8.25 - eight day

    The lovely face of a woman graces the lower part of the case. Her features are classical in design. Minerva was the Goddess of Wisdom, War, Learning, Arts and Crafts and Industry. She is one of the twelve Olympian Gods, and her symbol was the owl. As a Roman goddess she was known as Minerva, but as a Greek goddess she was known as Athena. Her city was Athens and she is depicted wearing a helmet.

    At the Roman Baths in Bath, England, the head of the statue Minerva shows the helmet and the owl, two of her symbols. We visited this magnificent archeological wonder.

    Daniel Chester French's sculpture of the goddess Minerva "Alma Mater" has become a symbol of Columbia University. More interesting, however, is that the goddess Minerva is a symbol for America. She is depicted on the Medal of Honor, holding the shield of the United States.

    A Seth Thomas movement is used in this model.

Minerva

LADY AND CHILD

Number:	143
Height:	19"
Movement:	8 day time & strike
Catalogs:	1874 - 76
Patent:	A. P.
Price:	1875 - $15.50

"Lady and Child" is a classic two major piece Müller clock. It was probably designed during Nicholas Müller's lifetime and finally patented and produced shortly after his death. Both Kroeber and Muller movements have been found in this model. Festoons and scrolls are used in a graceful manner and it features unusual feet. The figures are classically draped and posed.

When I look at this clock, I think about mother and child, so I am including a few quotes about mothers.

"To a child's ear "mother" is magic in any language".

"Being a full time mother is one of the highest salaried jobs, since the payment is pure love".

"For a mother is the only person on earth who can divide her love among 10 children and each child still still have all of her love."

"The most important thing a father can do for his children is to love their mother".

Lady and Child

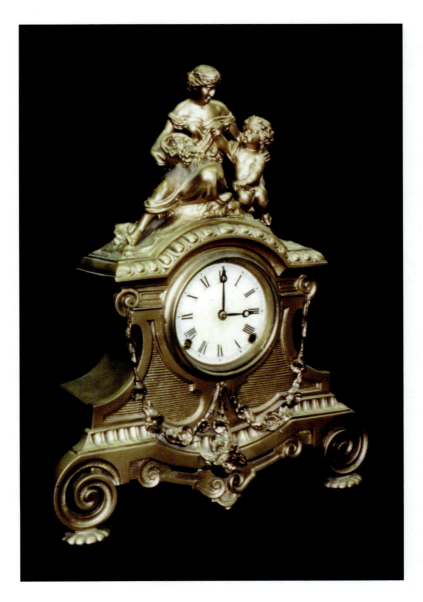

VICTORY

Number:	148
Height:	15"
Movement:	One day time & strike
Catalogs:	1872 - 76
Patent:	
Price:	1874 - $6.00

    The lines of this case show both elegance and simplicity. Although there are some elements that resemble the traditional Müller motifs, there are newer, more modern incised parts of the case that are innovative decorative "trends" that lend themselves to the changes in furniture designs of the day.

    Victory is something that we savor and desire to experience. The Olympian athlete, crowned with a wreath of leaves, has always been an inspiration. Whether it involves the victorious legions of Roman soldiers, the landings on the beaches of Normandy or something as simple as a baby's first steps, victory is satisfying and exciting.

    Although this case is not inspirational, it is beautifully crafted and conveys positive emotions. It is a reminder of a basic need – success – victory.

Victory

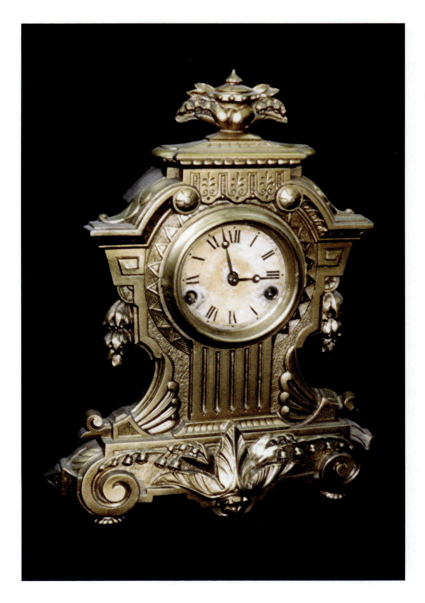

EGYPTIAN WITH BUST

Number:	150
Height:	17"
Movement:	8 day time & strike
Catalogs:	1874 - 1876
Patent:	
Price:	1874 - $18.50

    This is another Egyptian themed clock made in two completely separate pieces. The top bust is not attached to the base, so it is likely that this may have been mislaid or lost in many models. It is essential that you have both pieces, or the value will be greatly diminished.

    Things were changing worldwide in the last quarter of the 19th C. The great pyramid of Giza (built by Khufu in the 4th dynasty) was no longer the largest structure in the world. Verdi wrote the Egyptian themed opera "Aida" to premiere in Cairo in 1871.

    Since 1881, the obelisk known as "Cleopatra's Needle" has stood in New York City's Central Park, directly behind the Metropolitan Museum of Art. Tarot cards were introduced showcasing many Egyptian themes.

    The Egyptian Revival was a great marketing tool for the Müller Company.

Egyptian with Bust

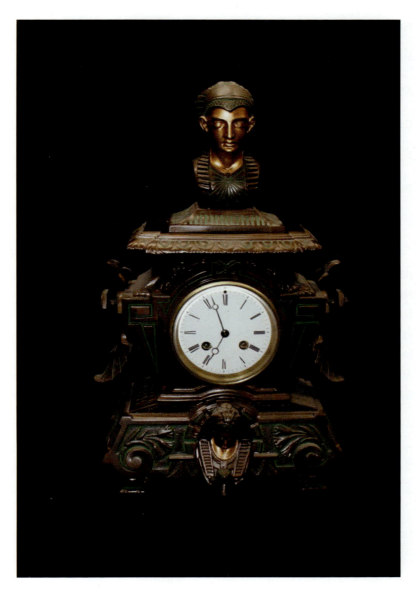

POCAHONTAS

Number:	161A
Height:	19 ½"
Movement:	8 day time & strike
Catalogs:	1874 - 1876
Patent:	
Prices:	1874 - $14.50

    The base, with its Indian heads was sold by E.N. Welch as "Dexter", #161 and featured a horse on the top piece. The Village of Dexter was founded in 1824 and was on the "Underground Railroad" for slaves escaping from the South. In 1869, the Cairo, Arkansas and Texas Railroad Company started building a line now known as "Cat Line" which ran near Dex Creek. A man named Webb owned a farm on its banks. He raised a fine racehorse and called him Dexter after the name of the creek. This horse, one of the most famous racehorses of its time, won many of his races in the area.

    When the top featured two birds on the same base, it was then named "Pocahontas" – 161A. Pocahontas (1595 - 1617) was a North American Indian princess, reputed to have saved Captain John Smith from execution. The Indian heads are also appropriate to the name of the clock.

Pocahontas

CHAPEL

Number:	162
Height:	13"
Movement:	8 day time & strike
Catalogs:	1874 - 1876
Patent:	A. P.
Prices:	1874 / 75 $13.25

This is a rather basic model, probably designed by the sons (most likely Herman). It is characteristic of the simpler, neater Eastlake design and no longer features the elaborate designs favored by Nicholas, who strongly appealed to Victorian tastes.

It is interesting to compare this clock with a similar clock, "Ruin" - # 120. During this period, even the simplest clock front was richly embellished overall. The clocks with numbers starting at 140 are not as artistic – no flowing lines – Art Deco looking rather than Art Nouveau – reflecting the changing tastes of the population.

The definition of chapel is that of church. The most famous chapel that comes to mind is one we visited a few years back. The Sistine Chapel ceiling contains the most perfect works done by Michelangelo. It is interesting to note that he resisted the commission to paint the ceiling, as he always considered himself to be a sculptor. What a loss it would have been to the world if he had persevered in his refusal.

Chapel

STUDY

Number:	163
Height:	14"
Movements:	8 day time & strike and one day time & strike
Catalog:	
Patent:	1876
Prices:	1874 - $7.50 - 8 day
	1874 - $6.25 - 1 day

    The graceful top of this clock, a one piece, two bezel model, features draperies and tassel may be a reflection of the decorative elements of the late Victorian period. The two figures, one on either side of the lower bezel, are not alike, yet harmonize with one another. They are classically draped and appear in repose. This clock contains an American Clock Co. movement.

    It is architectural, typical of the sons – yet highly reflective of the period. We have arbitrarily left this example in its base metal I do not believe that the Company offered any of its cases in this manner. We enjoy the variety of finishes we have chosen, as do those owners who choose to paint them in a "natural" manner.

Study

ORIENTAL

Number:	165
Height:	17"
Movement:	1874 - 1876
Patent:	1873
Prices:	1874 - $8.25

This case is definitely Asian in style – Oriental or Arabic. We first saw this clock in the home of our friend, Jules Weinberg, who introduced us to the NAWCC and to clock collecting. After seeing this clock, I was determined to own it and was finally able to acquire it, 15 years after first seeing it, when Jules and Helen moved from our neighborhood to Lake Placid. Jules never parted with a clock, although at the time he had over 2,000 of them. At the time of the move, he donated 200 clocks to the NAWCC Museum. We were fortunate that he really didn't fancy this particular clock.

It is garishly painted and bejeweled, having been most likely used in a Lodge such as the Shriners, or by an Asian or Arabic family. The numbers on the dial have been changed, as may be seen in the photograph. This was certainly done by a knowledgeable amateur.

We never found another example of this model, but are sure that there is one somewhere that must look very different from this one.

Oriental

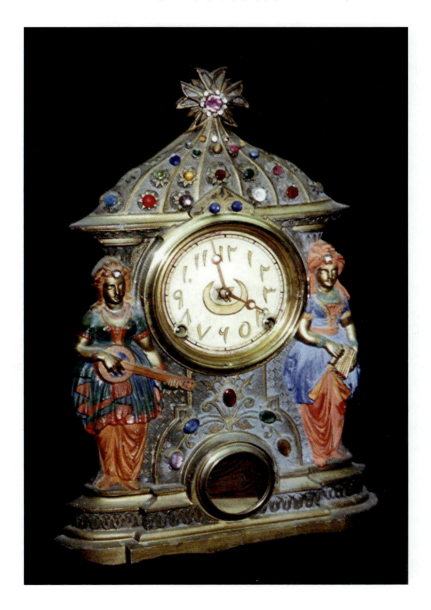

ROMANCE

Number:	166
Height:	21"
Movement:	8 day time & strike
Catalogs:	1874 - 1880
Patent:	1873
Prices:	1874 - $17.75

"Romance" resembles several large models which have deco-like bases, (Ulysses, Music and the Indian Hunter), however it has a more classical base. It seems as if the base on this clock was done by one person and the others mentioned above done by another. The statue features a classically garbed figure with flowing garments and graceful lines.

As may be seen in the last few listings, the prices of the clocks have risen slowly but steadily. This, I would guess, is because the economy of the late nineteenth century showed steady improvement.

Shakespeare and Kierkegaard share a similar viewpoint that marriage and romance are not harmoniously in tune with each other. Perhaps that is the reason that so many marriages fail. It has been said that we all need a little romance in our lives. Maybe we also need a little effort in our marriages.

Romance

ULYSSES

Number:	167
Height:	22 ½"
Movement:	8 day time & strike
Catalogs:	1874 - 1880
Patent:	1876
Prices:	1875 - $18.25

Ulysses, the Latin equivalent of the Greek, Odysseus, was the King of Ithaca, a Greek island. He was one of the Greek leaders in the Trojan War. He is shown with a bow and is elevated on the case to show importance and royalty.

The lower part of the case includes sides and the embellishment is late Victorian in style. Eastlake made furniture with incised designs, rather than raised elements. This example was assembled with a Kroeber movement.

"Ulysses" is similar in styling to "Music" and "Indian Hunter", in that its base is more Art Deco than those that were produced earlier. It is also important that the bow, an element that could easily have snapped off, still is in place. Once again, the missing part will affect value.

Ulysses

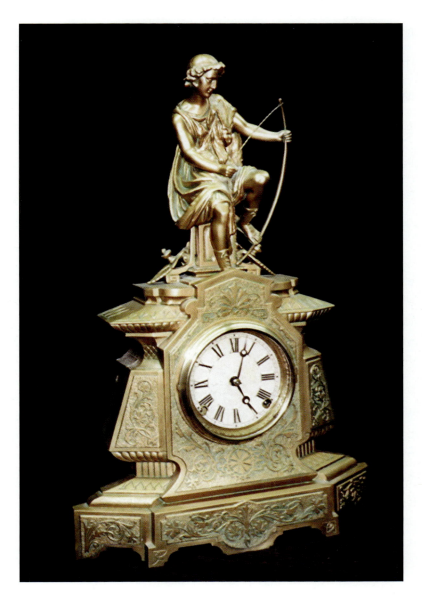

BOUQUET

Number:	170
Height:	9 ½"
Movement:	Lever – 1 day time & strike
Catalogs:	1874 - 1876
Patent:	
Price:	1874/75 - $6.50

Müller designed cases that were appropriate for their use with lever movements. They were quite small, in comparison with the majority of the designs the firm usually produced. Terry lever movements were found in these clocks ("Lady", "Innocence" and "Boy with Dog"). "Bouquet" most closely resembles the style of the black mantel clocks of the 1880's and 1890's.

This clock is unusual in that it incorporates an oval porcelain disc which, according to the catalogs I have seen, was hand painted with a bouquet of flowers. In the example shown here, the design had totally worn off the porcelain, perhaps from over-cleaning, and a paper print was glued atop the oval disc. If a clearer picture of the clock had been available to me, it would have been simple to paint a copy of the original image.

Bouquet

MUSIC

Number:	172
Height:	22"
Movement:	8 day time & strike
Catalogs:	1875 - 1880
Patent:	1874
Prices:	1875 - $18.25

    This case appears to be part of a series of classical figures atop late Victorian bases. Among similar clocks may be found "Ulysses" and "Indian Hunter". These use the late Victorian incised style of decoration.

    Once again, the central figure is classically garbed in the mode of the early Greeks and Romans. Although one example we found had a Waterbury movement, another was powered by a movement by N. Müller & Sons.

    What is music? Music can make us think, feel and act. It can be a deeply meaningful and profound experience. It is beauty, love and expression and every emotion you could dream of. You can relate to it – it resonates in your soul.

    It contains all of those memories of your youth, or that first dance.

Music

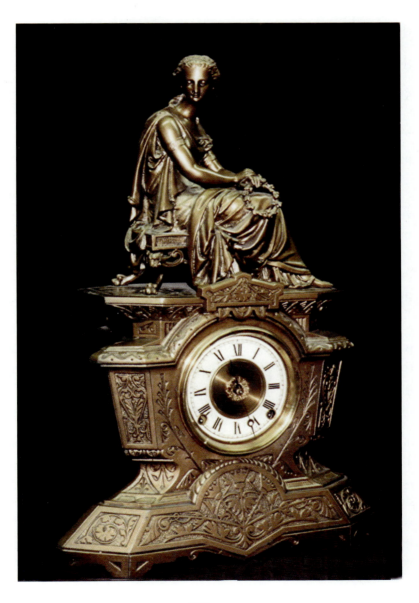

INDIAN HUNTER

(A/K/A) Chingachgook)

Number:	181
Height:	22"
Movement:	8 day time & strike
Catalog:	1885 – top figure only
Patent:	1880

 According to The Historical Society of Cooperstown, New York, a very similar statue "The Indian Hunter" (with his dog) was executed in bronze by John Quincy Adams Ward, a famous American sculptor. He conceived the idea in 1858 and completed it in 1886. It won a prize in a Paris exhibit. The original stands in Central Park in New York City and a duplicate on Otsego Lake in Cooperstown, in upstate New York.

 Representing an Indian of life size, one hand holding the bow from which he has just discharged an arrow, the other resting upon and restraining his dog,. His earnest gaze fixed upon the distant animal he has been hunting, it typifies the literary achievement of the greatest writer of purely American romance, James Fenimore Cooper.

 Herman Müller was granted a patent on the design for this clock in 1880, seven years after his father's death. The figure on the clock case appears to be identical to the Ward statue, which preceded it. Although, during Nicholas' lifetime, the company boasted that it had never copied the work of others, it would seem to be untrue in this case. Perhaps Ward gave permission for the duplication. Both Müller and the statue in Central Park were in New York City.

Indian Hunter

EGYPTIAN

Number: 183

Height: 19"

Movement: 8 day time & strike

Catalogs:

Patent:

Prices:

    Once again, this is an Egyptian themed model. Its styling resembles the wooden kitchen clocks popular during the last quarter of the 19th century, (the "gingerbreads"). It has a front opening full-sized door, through which we can view the dial as well as the pendulum action.

    Since the early 19th century, the interest in ancient Egyptian civilization had been an important influence on art, architecture, jewelry, collectibles, furnishings and CLOCKS.

    In the ancient Egyptian world, jewelry was worn to protect the wearer from evil. (I wear my Egyptian ankh whenever I travel). The Art Nouveau style borrowed greatly from Egyptian themes. For a brief period in America this was all the rage and highly prized.

    We have restored it in verde green, which was just one of the various finishes offered by the firm. The verde coloring is said to have been used to resemble the corrosive effect on copper. This model is equipped with a movement by N. Müller's Sons.

Egyptian

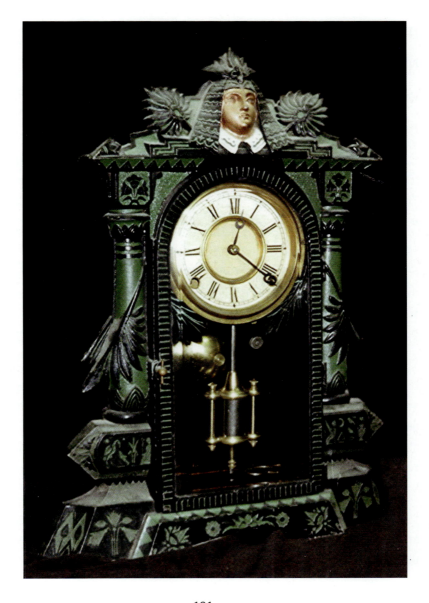

NEPTUNE

Number: 208

Height: 9"

Movement: 8 day lever movement

Catalogs: 1865 - 74

Patent:

One of the last clocks that I have acquired is this one – "Neptune". It is an unusual model, as it is a desk type model – lightweight and portable. The lever movement gives the owner the flexibility to move the clock more easily than if it were a pendulum model.

When the back of the clock is examined, we can clearly see rather confusing information. At the lower back of the case you will see clearly marked – "N. Müller's Sons & Co. No. 8. Just one inch to the right you will see "Cortlandt St. No. 208". The Müller firm was located at Cortlandt Street during the latter part of its existence but why the two different numbers?

At this point, I do not understand why there is disparity between the numbers. In the case of the policeman, the name of the company that special ordered the clock may be clearly seen along with their own number, as well as Müller's name. In this case, the above mentioned markings are clearly seen and only the Müller identification is there. Although it would seem to be highly unlikely that the No. 8 was an error, it is a possibility.

This casting is a charming representation of seamen and joins "Sailor" in its nautical styling and appeal. The seamen are not static but appear to be laboring at the wheel. The "umlaut" (German) is still being used in the Müller name.

Neptune

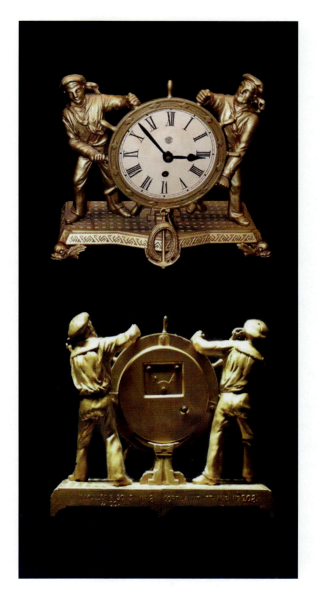

PALLAS

Number: 228

Height: 11 ¾"

Movement: 8 day time & strike

Catalogs:

Patent:

Prices:

Pallas – a Greek myth or Pallas Athena – so named by H. Wm. Oebers (1758 – 1840), a German astronomer, after the Greek goddess, the second asteroid discovered (1802) and the second largest (380 miles in diameter). Take your choice of the meaning of the name of the model.

This clock was made with a porcelain dial and French sash, with imitation marble or plush body, (this model shown here is the latter). It makes a perfect base for various statues.

The figure shown here was purchased by us with the clock, but any signed Müller figure would be appropriate.

Pallas

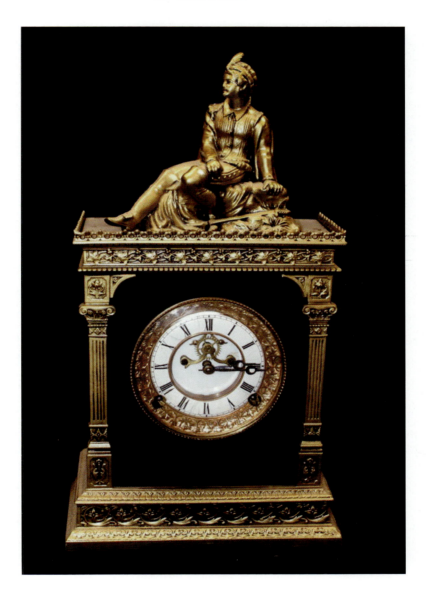

BEE

Number: 241

Height: 12"

Movement: 8 day time & strike

Catalogs: 1885

Patent:

Prices:

    In my opinion, this is a particularly beautiful clock and quite different from the entire production line. It has a hammered finish and, as it is illustrated, was offered with matching urns, for which I have been searching for a very long time. In the 1885 catalog are also shown very unique oil lamps with hammered finishes that would complement the clock.

    The case is made in the shape of a bee's body and the texture is reminiscent of the texture of the honey combs in the interior of the hive. Very innovative!

    This model is fitted with a porcelain dial with an outside escapement. It is shown in our very rare 1885 catalog offered by Nicholas Müller & Son, as well as many advertisements in the Jeweler's Circular and Horological Review.

Bee

AUGUR

Number:	247
Height:	10 ¼"
Movement:	8 day time & strike on ½ hour
Catalog:	1885
Patent:	

    The Augur was a priest and official in the classical world, especially Ancient Rome and Etruria. His main role was to interpret the will of the Gods by studying the flight of birds: whether they are flying in groups/alone, what noises they make as they fly, direction of flight and what kind of birds they are. This was known as "taking the auspices".

    The ceremony and function of the augur was central to any major undertaking in Roman society – public or private – including matters of war, commerce and religion. Their role was essential.

    The augur does not predict "what" course of action should be taken, but through his augery he finds signs on whether or not a course "already decided upon" meets with divine sanction and should proceed.

    Only some species of birds could yield valid signs, whose meaning would vary according to the species. Among them were ravens, woodpeckers, owls, and oxifragae eagles.

    The Müller Company showed a stylized bird at each side of the case. The figure shown in the ad shows the addition of a statue on top – probably the augur. It is unclear to me if the statue is free standing or if a specific top was attached to the case.

Augur

POLICEMAN

Number:	1102 (unlike any Müller identification)
Height:	17"
Copyright:	1889
Catalogs:	D. Buchner & Co. Tobacconists
Price:	Redeemed coupons

For obvious reasons, this is an extremely popular, sought-after model. Policemen exist and function throughout the world and are a very positive influence. This model is a very simple casting; it lacks a really professional flair and is a rather stereotypical rendering of a 19th century law enforcement officer.

The markings at the very bottom/back of the case have been quite confusing. Mr. Shawn thought that he was missing about nine hundred other cases. The number 1102 was not part of the Müller sequence and had some significance to the company that had placed the order.

This rendering of a police officer has brought auction results far above any other of the Mullers' production line, save for "The Ball Players". Baseball – The National Pastime appeals to the masses, as does the police officer.

My daughter, Allison, our very faithful researcher, finally solved the mystery of this clock. Please read on and find out the "whys" & "how's" & "where's".

Policeman

THE MYSTERY OF THE POLICEMAN CLOCK

D. Buchner & Company was a tobacco company in New York. It was one of the first companies to make baseball cards – from the mid 1800's to the early 1900's. These baseball trade cards were used for cigarette pack "stiffeners" and to boost sales.

In addition to baseball cards, they made other series of collectible cards – as "Police Inspectors and Captains" and "American Scenes with a Policeman". The company also issued a book entitled "Defenders and Offenders", glorifying Police Superintendents and Inspectors. They also issued cards for Jockeys and Actors.

As may be seen, the back sides of the Police Inspectors & Captains cards suggest that the purchaser should continue to save cards & wrappers as they are valuable. On the reverse of the "Scenes with a Policeman" card you will find a short list of premiums offered for the redemption of specific numbers of cards. The top prize was the Policeman clock "One of the Finest" for 600 cards.

Today each individual card is selling on E-Bay for more than one thousand dollars. Had they known, they could have kept the cards and been able to buy many, many clocks. (What is it that they say about hindsight?)

It would be great to find the runner-up prize – "One of the Bravest" - (a standing bronze finished figure) - the slogan of the New York City Fire Department . (The slogan of The New York City Police Department is "One of the Finest"). It would be logical to assume that this figure was also a Müller & Son product. The marking "Buchner & Co." may be clearly seen next to the Müller & Sons identification at the rear of the clock base.

By the late 1890's, Buchner merged with other tobacco companies to form "The American Tobacco Co".

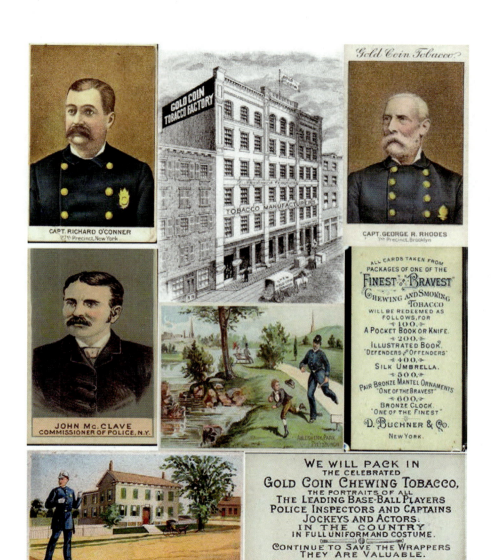

The D. Buchner Factory - Tobacco Manufacturer and Cards

Double Statue Clock

We were unaware that Müller made statue clocks until we saw one on display at a National Convention exhibit many years ago. That one was a single statue on the typical flat black platform, with a clock at the other end. Before we could find a single, a double came into our lives.

The finish is wonderful – it is the closest we have come to find what most closely resembles the original look. The statues are perfect, weapons and flag original and intact. The warriors are both signed on their rears, as is the clock 21 ½" wide by 19" high.

Double Statue Clock

Our second double statue Müller was purchased recently in "as is" condition. Since my husband 's health has deteriorated and he is incapable of doing any clock work at all, it will remain that way until another hobbyist takes over its restoration. Double statues were produced in the latter quarter of the 19th century and, due to their very large size they are worth more than singles. Few collectors have the physical space to collect them in large numbers, therefore fewer were sold and their rarity makes them more valuable.

Ink Wells

Courtesy of American Clock and Watch Museum.

A very similar inkwell was found is our 1885 Nicholas Mullers' Sons catalog. It was numbered 210 and called Jupiter. The picture shows that a clock was added to the double inkwell on an elevated shaft. Interestingly enough, the Museum inkwell is also signed Müller and numbered 201.

"Nickel and Bronze, cut glass ink bottle." The sphynx-like figures were also made as decorative statues. In Müller's numerical system, this did not mean that it was made much later than the clocks, but rather in tandem with other production.

Bronze Wall Shelves

Müller and Sons made many decorative items, among them these shelves. They came in many sizes, as shown. The first shelf shown is called "Neptune".

MOVEMENTS FOUND IN MULLER CLOCKS

- American Clock Co.
- Ansonia
- Owen E. Clark
- Gilbert
- Jerome
- F. Kroeber
- New Haven
- N. M. S.
- N. Müller & Sons
- N. Pomeroy
- Seth Thomas
- Terhune & Edwards
- S. B. Terry
- U. S. Clock Co.
- Waterbury
- E. N. Welch

IDENTIFICATION AND SPECULATION

The clocks of Nicholas Müller and his various successor companies generally are easily identified. Because of the craftsmanship and originality of his work, Müller's place in the history of horology is in part due to the elaborate system of identification used on almost all of his work.

Clocks can be identified by incised lettering that includes his name, usually N. Müller, a number, often the date, New York and patent information or AP (patent applied for or pending).

His early clocks are incised Müller with an "umlaut" over the u. According to Webster, an umlaut is the diacritical mark (") placed over a vowel, especially in German, to change the sound of the vowel. The u (with " above it) is not pronounced like cup (short) but rather like ue (as in duel or like mule). Later, the umlaut mark disappeared in the signatures on the clock fronts. I would guess this was done to "Americanize" his name (such as my grandmother did) or to remove any confusion or hint of foreign bias. He could have changed the family name to Mueller, as well.

In the first of his castings he engraved his name and clock number on the backside of the casting. It was later moved to other locations. Many clocks were one piece fronts with only one opening for the dial and were marked under the dial pan, which necessitated removal of hands, bezel glass and dial pan. Other one piece fronts have two openings and the information may be found by simply opening the pendulum bob bezel.

In cases that have two major parts, the incising is either found under the clock dial pan, once again involving disassembly, or somewhere in the back of the decorative clock top. Some of these have interchangeable tops, enabling the purchaser to custom make his clock. It was possible to pick a favorite base and purchase that alone (such as Swan" when it was the base alone) or by adding a decorative top it changed its name to "Mountaineer".

In the assembly of these clock cases Müller sometimes made a clock base that offered several compatible decorative tops. Using a horse on top of #161 it is called "Dexter". When the identical base has two quail for the top statue it is now numbered 161A and named "Pocahontas".

There is another series of four different tops for an identical base. They all have the same cast front but different statues on top, giving each clock a different appearance and all have been given a different name. These are "Mustang", "Savoyard", "Amazon" and "Fanchon No. 2". Jim Shawn had the good fortune to find all four in the set. There are no markings of any kind on any of the four models. This might have been a special order.

There is some indication that Müller provided statuary for the statue clocks made by Ansonia and Seth Thomas. Jim Shawn mentioned that some of the size and number dies he found on the Seth Thomas cases were the same as the ones with Müller's name. The style of workmanship attests to Müller's craftsmanship.

We purchased a Kroeber statue clock and had it for years. It took up a great deal of space on our shelves, so we decided to sell it at a National Convention. It featured a lady with a dove, marked only with Kroeber's name. A few months after we sold it, we visited the NAWCC Museum in Columbia and found a display cabinet prominently showing the very same clock, along with the patent applications signed by our favorite, Nicholas Müller. We have never been able to obtain another. Many companies did not wish to credit anyone but themselves for even a part of the clock.

We were unaware that Müller made any statue clocks, (a long metal base with a free-standing clock and a figure at the opposite end of the base) until we attended another National and saw one on display. This then opened another area that we had not explored. The Müller or NMS (Nicholas Müller's Sons) signature can be found inscribed into the backs of the statues and sometimes on the clock case itself. We now own two double statue Müller clocks.

In our quest for different Müller castings, it was often quite a "treasure hunt". Sometimes I bought one without any obvious markings, only to find that information in a very inconspicuous area. Many of the castings were so obviously examples of his work that they were added to the collection. In the 1970's and 80's we often shipped the fronts to Jim Shawn for his opinion, which almost always agreed with my "gut feelings".

There are a few outstanding castings that do not seem to have ever been marked, (The Highlander, for example). Perhaps the clock company using these castings had a reason for these omissions. The old catalogs showed them side-by-side in the collection of Müller clocks currently available.

Once the sons made the business their own, after Nicholas' death, the look of the fronts changed. The newer cases have none of the deep, artistic character of the older castings. Some models employ the front doors characteristic of the late 19th Century "new model" kitchen clocks, (always in the same pewter-like alloy). They used beveled glass, creating a large opening below the dial, through which the pendulum and bell could be viewed. Some of the later models also used porcelain dials with outside escapements. (See the "Bee" and "Augur").

The Eastlake style of furniture emerged during the last quarter of the Victorian Era and was reflected in many of the later Müller & Sons clocks. Rather than the ornate, sensuous flowing forms of the earlier Victoriana, Eastlake ornamented his furniture with the "modern" of the period: incised, rather than curved – geometric, more linear, neater. (See "Ulysses", "Indian Hunter" and "Music")

By the early 1880's, styles of clocks were changing even more and, in order to compete in the marketplace, Nicholas Müller's Sons was changing as well. The imitation marble black mantel clocks had become all the rage.

We have an original copy of the Nicholas Mullers' Sons 1885 catalog and in it they maintain the same numbering system as before. The typical Müller designs seem to have changed, beginning with the late #180's, and became instead the imitation marble clocks shown in the following reprints, with the occasional composition bronze ornate clock. (See "Pallas", the "Bee", "Augur" and "Policeman".) The imitation black mantel clocks were signed, numbered and named. (See the examples below on this page).

In addition to clocks, the catalog shows statuary, many the same figures that had been used on the tops of earlier clocks. Among the most familiar ones are "Wine Drinker", "Music", "Romance", and "Indian Hunter". Most were very classical in design. New desk models featured ink wells, many featuring thermometers or small clocks, some of which had calendar movements.

In business, it is important to stay current or even to anticipate trends in order to be successful. Since Herman was the only son running the production end of the business, the black imitation marble clocks would seem to require less artistic ability in both design and execution and therefore probably could be produced at lesser cost and with fewer specialized workers. Profit, after all, has always been the driving force.

SOUDAN.—No. 221.
IMITATION MARBLE.
MADE ALSO IN COLORED (RED) MARBLE.

Height, 15 inches.
Cut illustrates
8 day, ½ hour strike, gong. Porcelain Dial, French Sash.

TUNIS.—No. 225 B.
IMITATION MARBLE.
MADE IN COLORED (RED AND BLACK) MARBLE.

Height, 10½ inches.
Cut illustrates 8 day, ½ hour strike.
Visible Escapement, French Sash and Dial.

SUEZ.—No. 227 B.
IMITATION MARBLE.

Height, 11 inches.
Cut illustrates 8 day, ½ hour strike.
Visible Escapement, Patent Regulating Attachment,
French Sash and Dial.

CORINTH.—No. 196.
IMITATION MARBLE.

Height, 11½ inches.
Cut illustrates 8 day, ½ hour strike.
Visible Escapement, French Sash and Dial.

SPARTA.—No. 222.
IMITATION MARBLE.
MADE ALSO IN RED, BLACK AND COLORED MARBLE.

Height, 11 inches.
Cut illustrates
8 day, ½ hour strike, gong. Porcelain Dial, French Sash.

IMITATION MARBLE CLOCKS

RESTORATION

Although modern restoration practices and preferences dictate that restoration of antiques should be reversible and as minimal as possible, in the matter of these metal clocks restoration invariably must be done. Having been manufactured in the mid to late nineteenth century, time has taken its toll. For close to 150 years, they have been subjected to what my Appraisal Studies Professor, Dr. Sigmund Rothschild, called "good housewifeliness". Cleaning, dusting, polishing and handling have caused the finish to rub away and encouraged owners to paint and overpaint with "gold radiator paint". This overpainting, in turn, often obliterated the exacting detail of the original castings.

When starting to "bring the clock back to life", it is necessary to disassemble the entire clock, setting aside the wooden box holding the movement, as well as the bezels, glass and other components, to be worked on at another time. The metal case fronts usually need work.

My husband, George, experimented with almost every available paint stripper over these almost forty years, finally being pleased with a commercial grade industrial stripper. Layer after layer, the finish has to b e removed and cleared out of every crevice and tiny opening in the casting. He used various tools to clean out and unclog areas so vital to the details of the artist's work … ice picks, screw drivers, paint scrapers, steel wool and anything else that would accomplish the task. This part of the job is not completed until every tiny bit of the old finish is gone. The case is then washed and allowed to dry thoroughly. It is usually better to allow a full 24 hours to fully dry before proceeding with the refinishing.

Once again, it was necessary to experiment with every metallic spray paint or finish available in our area (including New York City). Often we found a wonderful finish, only to find that the line had been discontinued. The best we were able to find was a product called "Plater's Spray", offering various tones and shades of metallic finishes.

The entire case must then be lightly sprayed, allowing for drying between coats –often using darker, richer or lighter tones to highlight areas where it was needed. The finishing color is a matter of taste, but should please you. Allow to dry, once again. We did try to make the earlier clocks in the Bronze finish that was offered at that time. Later cases offered a small variety of colors and we were happy to experiment with what we thought was the right shade for the different cases.

After the case dried once again, we used Tinting Black, which is available in well established hardware and paint stores. A small amount of the well mixed black should be put into a baby food (or the like) jar, and a slight amount of water added and stirred. The medium should be neither too thick nor too thin. Paint right over the bronze finish – all over it – and allow it to partially dry for a short time. Gently rub overall with soft cloths, removing the black from the larger areas and leaving it in the crevices and openings. Work while the tinting black is still semi-moist and malleable. Do not work too energetically, as you may end up removing the bronze as well as the black. You can re-apply the tinting black in areas that do not please you. Like my grandmother's cooking, there are no precise measurements for this. The ultimate result should be pleasing and meet your expectations.

This coat is essential to avoid the garish look that the casting will take on after using the metallic paint spray. Leaving the black in the crevices makes your work look "antique" and mellow to the eye. The final coat is an overall spray with clear matte polyurethane to seal. This coat is also essential since, with time, the gold tends to darken too much. The poly also adds longevity to the finish of the clock.

As to the colors of the finishes used in different decades of the company, we have catalogs that show that Nicholas Müller offered these clock cases in

"Composition Bronze" at the beginning of his career and until his death, with the sons offering several choices during the later years of the company.

The following is a paragraph found in The Jeweler's Circular and Horological Review, dated October 21st, 1891:

"The celebrated finish known as the Electrical French Bronze was introduced by Nicholas Müller. This has a rich brazen or gold tinge, formed by a plating of bronze so heavy as to allow of oxidation. Another noticeable finish of this firm's production is the Barbedienne, named after the famous real bronze manufacturer of Paris. This finish has an earthen tinge and allows an admirable play of light and shade, thus permitting all the details of the piece to be readily seen. Again there is the Japanese finish, copper-ish in tinge and oxidation, the Dark Japanese, the Polished Brass, and numerous others depending upon the versatility and skill of the plater".

This information has helped us to choose colors of finishes that we have used on clocks made in specific time periods during the years in which Müller and his successors worked.

There are several companies around the country offering electroplating of these cases. They offer several different tones of the bronze finish, as did the company itself. The results are wonderful and certainly worth the prices charged. We have had a few of our cases professionally done and are most delighted with the results.

We have seen castings that have been painted "realistically" - that is – green for the leaves, purple for the grapes, flesh tone for the skin, etc. This was never offered in any catalogs, reprints or lists that we have seen. This type of refinishing obviously pleased the owners of the clocks at that time and place, but certainly did not mimic the finish that Müller had intended. He was, after all, a maker of bronze statuary and his work reflected the European tastes and sensibilities of the 19th Century.

The owner of The Old Clock Museum in Pfarr, Texas, chose to over paint many of his cases in this "realistic" (my choice of word) manner. Some of the clocks that we have seen, decorated in this manner, are actually quite attractive, however. As long as this type of restoration is reversible (paint can be removed and finish restored to the original look), no harm has been done to the integrity of the piece. You will find several realistically painted fronts in the section showing the clocks. Several are shown immediately adjacent to the same clock front finished in a "bronzier" finish. It is your choice to determine which is more pleasing.

We have kept a few of our clocks in the base metal – after all paint was removed we simply sealed the casting with polyurethane. These clocks seem to add a dimension to the collection and show the front in great detail.

Often we found a desirable front that happened to be missing parts or components – pieces of the design missing. There are also many case fronts to be found (lacking movements, dials, bezels and the wooden supports of various kinds that make up the case). These create various problems for the restorer. My husband loved the challenge of rebuilding the entire clock "from scratch". The results can be amazing!

It helps to have as many examples of Müller's work as we do. In the case of small components that are missing, it is helpful that he often repeated the same small trims, flowers, garlands and .other embellishments. My husband was able to make molds of the original parts by using clay from my Kindergarten classroom, pressing the original piece firmly into the clay and removing it carefully. He then was able to fill the impression left with commercially available liquid metal. He experimented with many different products, as some were better than others. After the small pieces hardened thoroughly, he filed, chipped away and sculpted, making the pieces as close to the original as possible. The piece was then finished in the same manner as the front and glued in place, allowing the replacement part to "melt" into the complete front.

When I purchased "Fisher Boy and Dog", everything was great except that the string of fish shown in the catalogs was missing from his hand. The reprinted catalog was not too clear in showing small details, but George was finally able to duplicate the fish to a wonderful degree. It took many evenings at his bench to accomplish this. He was extremely pleased, as was I. About a year later, I located another "Fisher Boy & Dog", but this one had the original string of fish! After several hours spent comparing the two clocks, he announced that we were keeping the first clock, "because", he announced, "my fish are better than his." The more original clock found a new owner and we still have "Fisher Boy and Dog with the Very Best Fish".

Another problem occurred when we obtained "The Goat", one of my personal favorites. The entire clock was perfect, save for the fact that his right horn was broken off and missing. Try as he may, my husband was unable to create a satisfactory replacement for the right horn. He finally settled on recasting the left horn and attaching it perfectly to the missing area on the head. He then announced that we now owned the only goat in the world with two left horns. It remains one of my favorite examples of Müller's expertise as a sculptor. I am sure that, except for the occasional goat farmer, and without this revelation, no one will ever notice.

At meetings, we were able to pick up movements similar to the ones used in the Müller clocks.   They are pictured here.

Muller 8 day Time & Strike marked N. Muller

Muller 8 day Time & Strike Open Escapement

Unmarked 8 day Time & Strike

The movements are back mounted strap movements made by the many manufacturers who used Müller cases. Jim Shawn made up his own set of instructions for building the boxes used to mount the movements which are encased in the finished clocks. I quote him almost verbatim:

"Take the works and lay them on the table top or any flat surface. Now take your casting and put it over the works with the hand shafts elevated through the dial hole enough for the hands to be in the proper position; then take some books and block up under the casting till the straight rib on the back of the casting is the same distance from the table top at all points. This will give you the width of the side boards of your case if the back board is screwed to the back. If recessed into the side boards you will have to add the thickness of the board to the width of your side boards to hold your hand shaft distance correct. Now on the back of the casting we will find three or four lugs slightly to one side of the rib that the box fits against. We shall drill a small hole out near the end of them; these are for the screws to hold the box to the front. One more thing about this box – it should have the back board or side boards extend down far enough to serve as legs at the back so clock will stand up straight".

Bezels and glass of the same period are often available at local, regional and national meetings and marts. The most difficult to find have always been the small pendulum opening bezels used on most of the one piece fronts. We were able to find Vincent Versage, of upstate New York, who had a fabulous machine shop where he spun precise bezels for those clocks missing that part. Since his death, we have had to find old ones at meetings. On occasion, we have actually purchased "a real wreck" just to obtain that elusive missing bezel.

My husband had always been extremely interested in woodworking and constructing furniture, so the boxes or backs necessary to assembling an entire Müller clock were relatively easy for him to figure out. The clocks that we have seen are of all sizes and shapes, but the mounting boxes are similar. Some are vertical and some relatively square or horizontal. The depth of the cases also varies, so the few wooden cases we have needed over the years were custom made by George.

Those mounting boxes are very true to the originals. He insisted on using old square nails, as were used in most of our absolutely original clocks. We were able to obtain fruit crates from local markets, and these were carefully disassembled. Different fruits are distributed in boxes made of different thicknesses of wood. It is difficult to obtain this type of wood from lumber yards.

Over these forty years of collecting, and myriads of marts, regionals and nationals, we have been fortunate to find and purchase a large number of Müller clocks, always keeping the best, most original example of each model. As in all collecting areas, originality is ultra important in these clocks but, in my opinion, leaving them "as found" is detrimental to their values. Movements, of course, must be in good repair, but the aesthetics of the entire clock must be considered.

I would certainly discourage any "marriages" (wrong tops on wrong bases), but do feel that the restoration discussed in the chapter enhances their values and adds to the enjoyment of owning and displaying them.

STATUES

In addition to clocks, shelves, and inkwells N. Muller also produced a vast number of figures (human and animals) and busts. Constructed from the same materials used in his clocks and other items their sizes varied from statues in excess of 10 inches in height to toppers which were used to adorn the imitation marble clocks. Below are various examples of his work.

PATENTS

Through the generosity of The Library & Research Center of NAWCC, I am in possession of many copies of original patents by Müller and his successors. According to Stacy B.C. Wood., Jr., former Museum director, he has examined the many patents in the Museum's holding and determined that, during the period of 1845-1887, at least 40 or more design patents were issued to or assigned to the brothers (Nicholas & Karl) or to Nicholas' three sons.

Although the patents were generally typed, there are two in this chapter that are hand-written in the cursive style. I have included these in this chapter, as they were of great interest to me. Unlike the handwriting of the present, the script shown is highly legible and consistent in its form.

Since Karl (or Carl) Müller, the very talented sculptor – brother and co-founder of the firm, returned to Europe in 1854, it seemed to be unlikely that he could have easily returned to patent many of his beautifully executed clock front designs. No record of this possibility exists.

In examining some of his patents it was clear that he had given his brother the power to patent many designs that he had left behind. The following phrase may be seen on many of his Patent applications: "Carl (sometimes Karl) Müller, assignor to Nicholas Müller". One other patent, among those that I have seen, was issued to: Peter B. Wight – Assignor to Nicholas Müller – dated March 5, 1871", just one year before Nicholas' death. Perhaps they felt the need to acquire designing skill, due to a possible health problem of Nicholas'. Wight's name is not further mentioned in the available records.

It seems practical to include in this section only patents of clocks not photographed and discussed in other parts of the book. This enables the reader to see drawings of other Müller designs, some of which appear to be rare. It may also aid the collector in finding the more unusual designs that he produced, as some of these may be difficult to identify, due to lack of the usual identifying marks.

NO, 52 LEATHER STOCKINGS

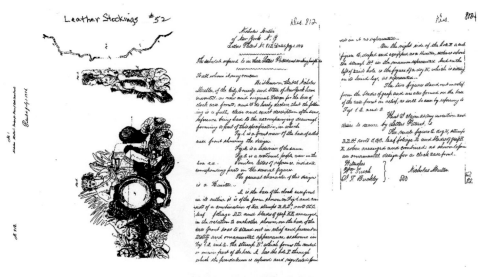

NO. 116 WINE DRINKER - BOTTOM

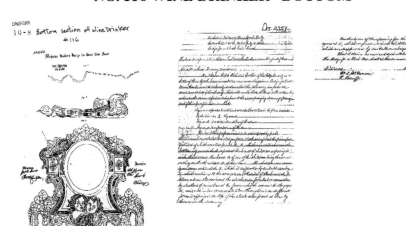

HANDWRITTEN PATENTS

Miner #137

Army and Navy

Nº 3249

Carl Müller's Design for a Clock Case

PATENTED
NOV 17 1868

Witnesses
Jno. W. Williams
Henry Kanya

Inventor
Carl Müller

DESIGNS
10-8

Nicholas Müller's Design for a CLOCK CASE
4237
PATENTED JUL. 19 1870

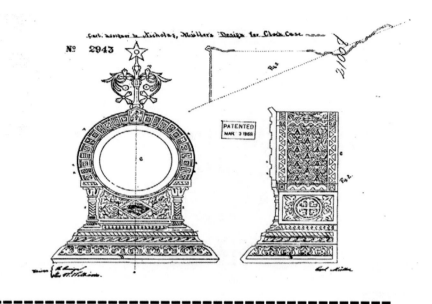

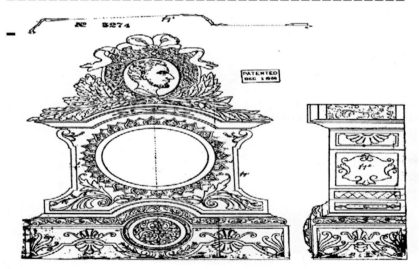

INDEX OF CLOCKS BY NAME

We are very fortunate indeed to have Chris Bailey's meticulously researched list of every Müller clock that was shown in any of the available catalogues of the years 1852 to 1880. Although some clocks were made after 1880, the bulk of the company's production was done during this time. As in all of his research, it is most accurate and has proven to be very helpful to me.

He has included the information about the sources that he used and I am so very grateful that he has permitted me to publish this compilation in my book. I know that it will be of use to generations of people who are admirers of the work of Nicholas Müller and his companies.

Many of these catalogues are stored in the annals of the American Clock and Watch Museum in Bristol, Connecticut. I was privileged to have examined a few very fragile originals, as well as many copies. There is so little information available about Müller that every thread weaves itself into the tapestry of his life and is very much appreciated.

Mr. Bailey is the recently retired curator and managing director of the Bristol Museum.

Compiled by Chris H. Bailey

1852 – Jerome & Co. Manufacturers and Wholesale Clock Dealers, No. 88 Market Street, corner of Third Street and No. 82 North Third Street, Philadelphia, 1852.

1853 – Chauncey Jerome, Manufacturer of Brass Clocks, New Haven, Conn. Wholesale Warehouses, No. 175 Broadway, No. 2 Cortland Street, New York. No. 73 Hanover Street, Boston. No. 6 New Quay, Liverpool, England.

1858 – Catalogue of American Clocks and Regulators, Manufactured by Gilbert, Hubbard & Co., at Winsted and Ansonia, Conn. Sales Room at 26 Liberty Street, New-York. (not dated, but probably 1858, possibly 1859.

1859 – New Haven Clock Co, Manufacturers of Brass Clocks, New Haven, Conn, 1859. (only 20 pages, may be incomplete).

1865 – American Clock Co, 3 Cortlandt St., New York & 115 Lake Street, Chicago. Nov. 1, 1865

1866 – Price list for the firm of Fuller & Kroeber, 25 John Street, New York, September, 1866

1867 – Illustrated Catalogue of Clocks, Regulators and Calendars, Manufactured and Sold by the Waterbury Clock Company, No. 4 Cortlandt Street, New York City, June 1867.

1869 – Illustrated Catalogue of Clocks, Manufactured by E. N. Welch Manufacturing Company and New Haven Clock Company, and the Leading Styles of Other Makers, Sold by American Clock Company, 3 Cortlandt Street, New York, 115 Lake Street, Chicago, 310 Sansome Street, San Francisco. Jan. 1, 1869

1872 – October, 1872. Illustrated Catalogue of the Most Salable Styles of American Clocks, of Reliable Manufacture sold by G. S. Lovell, Wholesale Clock Dealer, 627 Market Street, Philadelphia.

1874A – Ansonia Brass & Copper Co's Catalogue of Clocks. April, 1874A.

1874B – October, 1874. Illustrated Catalogue of the Most Salable Styles of American Clocks, of Reliable Manufacture, sold by G. S. Lovell, Wholesale Clock Dealer, 627 Market Street, Philadelphia. **This catalog had a retail price list.**

1874C – Illustrated Catalogue of Clocks, Manufactured by E. N. Welch Manufacturing Co., New Haven Clock Company, Welch, Spring & Company, and the Leading Styles of other Makers, Sold by American Clock Company, 581 Broadway, New York, 172 State Street, Chicago, 520 Market Street, San Francisco. September 1, 1874A.

1875 – Illustrated Catalogue of Clocks, Manufactured and Sold by the Waterbury Clock Co., New York, Chicago, San Francisco. July, 1875. **This catalog had a retail price list.**

1876 – Illustrated Catalogue of Clocks, Manufactured by the Seth Thomas Clock Company, New Haven Clock Company, E. N. Welch Manufacturing Company, Welch, Spring & Company, and the Leading Styles of Other Makers, sold by the American Clock Company, 583 Broadway, New York, 172 State Street, Chicago, 520 Market Street, San Francisco. May 1, 1876.

1880 – Illustrated Catalogue of Clocks Manufactured by F. Kroeber, Office and Salesroom, No. 8 Cortlandt Street, New York. [This catalog was not dated, but proven by models included to be the year 1880.]

Sizes: Some fronts came in two distinct sizes, often a 1-day clock was smaller than the 8-day counterpart. In some instances the two close sizes, usually a half inch, less difference, were given in various catalogs for a model, in which case we believe the fronts were the same, but just measured differently. When two close sizes are given, the size given most frequently is underlined.

* Behind a year denoted the model was listed in the price list for that year, but not illustrated in that year's trade catalog.

COMPOSITION (SPELTER) CASES

Muller
No.

35   Adam & Eve (18 inches) – 8D, T&S – 1858
     Alexis (15.5 inches) – 8D, T&S – 1874A, 1874B*, 1874C, 1875, 1876
         Price: 1874: $8.25, 1875: $8.25

229

104	Alhambra [called Large Alhambra in 1869] (14 inches) – 8D, T&S – 1869, 1874A, 1874B*, 1874C, 1875*, 1876 Price: 1874: $11.25, 1875: $11.25
none	Amazon (16 or 17 inches) – 8D, T&S – 1874A, 1874B*, 1874C, 1875, 1876 Price: 1874: $9.00, 1875: $9.00
111	Amour [Amor] (20 inches) – 8D, T&S – 1865, 1867, 1869, 1874A, 1874B*, 1874C, 1875, 1876 Price: 1874: $19.50, 1875: $19.50
	Angel Swing, No. 3 (19.5 inches) – 8D, T – 1880
	Angel Swing, No. 3 (19.5 inches) – 8D, T&S – 1880
109	Armorer (18 inches) – 8D, T&S – 1865, 1867, 1869, 1872, 1874A, 1874B, 1874C, 1875, 1876 Price: 1874: $13.50, 1875: $13.50
	Army and Navy (14 inches) – 8D, T&S – 1869
22	Artist (12 inches) – 8D, T – 1858
	Ball Players (16 inches) – 1D, T&S – 1869 Price: 1875: $7.00
135	Ball Players (16 inches) – 8D, T&S – 1869, 1874A, 1875 Price: 1875: $8.25
69	Beggar (16.5 inches) – 8D, T&S – 1872, 1874A, 1874B, 1874C, 1875, 1876 Price: 1874: $8.75, 1875: $8.75
59	Birds (21 inches) – 8D, T&S – 1858, 1867, 1874A, 1875 Price: 1875: $9.25
108B	Bird's Nest (18 inches) – 8D, T&S – 1874A, 1874B*, 1874C, 1875, 1876 Price: 1874: $9.75, 1875: $9.75
	Bourne (10 inches) – 8D, T&S – 1867
170	Bouquet (9.5 inches, lever mvt.) – 1D, T – 1874B, 1874C, 1875, 1876 Price: 1874: $6.00, 1875: $6.00
170	Bouquet (9.5 inches, lever mvt.) – 1D, T&S – 1874B, 1874C, 1875, 1876 Price: 1874: $6.50, 1875: $6.50
82	Boy and Dog (11 inches, lever mvt.) – 1D, T – 1867, 1869, 1872, 1874A, 1874B, 1874C, 1875, 1876 Price: 1874: $7.00, 1875: $7.00
82	Boy and Dog (11 inches, lever mvt.) – 1D, T&S – 1858, 1865, 1867, 1869, 1874A, 1874B, 1874C, 1875, 1876 Price: 1874: $7.50, 1875: $7.50
	Brilliant (16.5 inches) – 8D, T&S – 1880

81	Bronze [later called Mantel] (7 inches) – 1D, T – 1858
	Bronze Lever (9 inches, no model name) – 1D, T – 1853
	Bronze Lever Time Piece (no size or model name) – 1D, T – 1853
	Bronze Lever Time Piece. (no size or model name) – 1D, T – 1853
	Bronze Lever (round 5 inch diameter wall case, lever mvt.) – 1D, T – 1865, 1867, 1869
22	Calendar (with separate calendar in top) (22 inches) – 8D, T&S – 1858
23	Caryatide (15 inches) – 8D, T&S – 1858
133	Cathedral (14 inches) – 1D, T&S – 1869, 1874A, 1874B*, 1874C, 1875, 1876
	Price: 1874: $6.00, 1875: $6.00
133	Cathedral (14 inches) – 8D, T&S – 1874*, 1874C, 1875, 1876
	Price: 1874: $7.25, 1875: $7.25
40B	Ceres (14 inches) – 8D, T&S – 1858
158	Chapel (9.5 inches, lever mvt.) – 1D, T – 1874A, 1874B, 1874C, 1875, 1876
	Price: 1874: $6.50, 1875: $6.50
158	Chapel (9.5 inches, lever mvt.) – 1D, T&S – 1875
	Price: 1875: $7.00
158	Chapel (9.5 inches, lever mvt.) – 8D, T&S – 1874A
162	Chapel (13 inches) – 8D, T&S – 1874B, 1874C, 1875, 1876
	Price: 1874: $13.25, 1875: $13.25
122	Chase and Figure (21 inches) – 8D, T&S – 1867
74	Chase and Pantheon (22 inches) – 8D, T&S – 1858
	Cortland (18.25 inches) – 8D, T&S – 1880
57	Cupid (16 inches) – 1D, T&S – 1858, 1865, 1867, 1869, 1872, 1874A, 1874B, 1874C, 1875, 1876
	Price: 1874: $6.50, 1875: $6.50
57	Cupid (16 inches) – 8D, T&S – 1865, 1867, 1869, 1872, 1874B, 1874C, 1875, 1876
	Price: 1874: $7.75, 1875: $7.75
49	Cupid (18.5 inches) – 8D, T&S – 1858, 1865, 1867, 1869, 1872, 1874A, 1874B, 1874C, 1875, 1876
	Price: 1874: $9.00, 1875: $9.00
161	Dexter (19 or 19.25 inches) – 8D, T&S – 1874A, 1874B, 1874C, 1875, 1876, 1880
	Price: 1874: $13.50, 1875: $13.50
112B	Dog (16 inches) – 8D, T&S – 1874A, 1874B, 1874C, 1876
	Price: 1874: $10.50

61	Dolphin (20 inches) – 8D, T&S – 1858, 1865, 1867, 1869, 1872, 1874A, 1874B, 1874C, 1875, 1876 Price: 1874: $8.75, 1875: $8.75
	Domestic, V. P. (19.5 inches) – 8D, T&S – 1880
85	Dove [or Doves] (9 inches, lever mvt.) – 1D, T – 1865, 1869, 1874B*, 1874C, 1875, 1876 Price: 1874: $4.50, 1875: $4.50
85	Dove [or Doves] (9 inches, lever mvt.) – 1D, T&S – 1869, 1874B*, 1874C, 1876 Price: 1874: $5.00, 1875: $5.00
85	Doves (10 inches) – 8D, T – 1858
85	Doves (10 inches) – 1D, T&S – 1858
71	Drama (16 inches) – 1D, T&S – 1858, 1867, 1874A, 1875 Price: 1875: $8.75
71	Drama (16 inches) – 8D, T&S – 1858, 1867, 1874A, 1875 Price: 1875: $10.00
12	Dragon (15.5 inches) – 1D, T&S – 1867, 1872, 1874B, 1875*, 1876 Price: 1874: $4.75, 1875: $4.75
17	Dragon (15.5 inches) – 8D, T&S – 1858
112C	Drummer (18.5 inches) – 8D, T&S – 1865, 1867, 1869, 1872, 1874A, 1874B, 1874C, 1875, 1876 Price: 1874: $10.25, 1875: $10.25
54	Eagle (18.5 inches) – 8D, T&S – 1858, 1865, 1867, 1869, 1874A, 1874B*, 1874C, 1875, 1876 Price: 1874: $9.00, 1875: $9.00
138	Egyptian (10.75 inches) – 1D, T&S – 1874A, 1874C, 1875, 1876 Price: 1875: $4.75
138	Egyptian (10.75 inches) – 8D, T&S – 1874A, 1875 Price: 1875: $6.00
150	Egyptian with Bust (17 inches) [similar to below, but different added decorations] – 8D, T&S – 1874A, 1874B, 1874C, 1875*, 1876 Price: 1874: $18.50, 1875: $18.50
150	Egyptian, No. 150. (11 inches) [similar to above, but no bust and different added decorations] – 8D, T&S – 1874A, 1874C, 1875, 1876
	Esmeralda (18 inches) – 8D, T&S – 1874A, 1874B, 1874C, 1875, 1876 Price: 1874: $11.75, 1875: $11.75
	Etruscan No. 1 (18 inches) (Tucker bronze style cast metal dial) – 8D, T&S – 1867
118	Etruscan No. 1 (18 inches) (white [porcelain?] dial) – 8D, T&S – 1869, 1872, 1874A, 1874B*, 1874C, 1875, 1876 Price: 1874: $15.00, 1875: $15.00

	Etruscan No. 2 (18.5 inches) (Tucker bronze style cast metal dial) – 8D, T&S – 1867	
	Etruscan No. 2 (18.5 or 19 inches) (white [porcelain?] dial) – 8D, T&S – 1874A, 1874B*, 1874C, 1875, 1876	
	Price: 1874: $15.00, 1875: $15.00	
	Etruscan No. 3 (17 or 18 inches) – 8D, T&S – 1869, 1874A, 1874B*, 1874C, 1875, 1876	
	Price: 1874: $16.75, 1875: $16.75	
	Evangeline (19 inches) – 8D, T&S – 1865, 1867, 1869, 1872, 1874A, 1874B, 1874C, 1875, 1876, 1880	
	Price: 1874: $9.75, 1875: $9.75	
41	Evangelist (17 inches) – 1D, T&S – 1858, 1865, 1867, 1874A, 1874B*, 1875*, 1876	
	Price: 1874: $5.50, 1875: $5.50	
41	Evangelist (17 inches) – 8D, T&S – 1874A, 1874B*, 1876	
	Price: 1874: $8.75	
38	Evangelist (20 inches) – 8D, T&S – 1858, 1865, 1867	
	Falcon (16 inches) – 1D, T&S – 1865, 1869, 1874A	
	Falcon (16 inches) – 8D, T&S – 1874A	
none	Fanchon, No. 2 (17 or 18.5 inches) – 8D, T&S – 1874A, 1874B*, 1875*, 1876	
	Price: 1874: $8.75, 1875: $8.75	
70	Fisher Boy (19 inches) – 8D, T&S – 1858	
	Fisher Boy [New Style] (22.5 inches) – 8D, T&S – 1872, 1874A, 1874B, 1874C, 1875, 1876	
	Price: 1874: $16.75, 1875: $16.75	
93	Fisher Boy and Dog (18 inches) – 8D, T&S – 1865, 1867, 1869, 1872, 1874A, 1874B, 1874C, 1875, 1876	
	Price: 1874: $14.00, 1875: $14.00	
	Fox and Dog (10 inches, lever mvt.) – 1D, T – 1865, 1869, 1874B*, 1874C, 1875, 1876	
	Price: 1874: $5.50, 1875: $5.50	
65	Fox and Hare (19.75 inches) – 8D, T&S – 1858, 1865, 1867, 1869, 1874A, 1874B*, 1874C, 1875, 1876	
	Price: 1874: $9.50, 1875: $9.50	
	French (12 inches, lever mvt.) – 1D, T – 1874A	
	French (20 inches) [different from above] – 8D, T&S – 1865, 1867	
111C	Garabaldi (Garribaldi) (20.5 inches) [also called Victor Emmanuel in 1874A] – 8D, T&S – 1874A, 1874B*, 1874C, 1875, 1876	
	Price: 1874: $19.00, 1875: $19.00	
78	Garland (17 inches) – 8D, T&S – 1858	
112	Gleaner (17.75 or 18.5 inches) – 8D, T&S – 1865, 1867, 1869, 1872, 1874A, 1874B, 1874C, 1875, 1876	
	Price: 1874: $10.25, 1875: $10.25	

#	Description
84	Globe (19.5 or 20 inches) – 8D, T&S – 1858, 1865, 1867
	Goat (16 inches) – 8D, T&S – 1874A, 1874B*, 1874C, 1875 Price: 1874: $14.00, 1875: $14.00
21	Goat (18.5 inches) – 8D, T&S – 1865, 1869, 1872, 1876
	Gothic (16 or 16.25 inches) – 1D, T&S – 1865, 1867, 1869, 1872, 1874A, 1874B, 1875 Price: 1874: $5.50, 1875: $5.50
19	Gothic (18.5 or 19 inches) – 8D, T&S – 1858, 1865, 1867, 1869, 1872, 1874A, 1874B, 1875, 1876 Price: 1874: $7.25, 1875: $7.25
	Greek (14.5 inches) – 1D, T&S – 1872, 1874A, 1874B, 1875*, 1876 Price: 1874: $6.25, 1875: $6.25
	Greek (17 inches) – 8D, T&S – 1872, 1874A, 1874B, 1875*, 1876 Price: 1874: $9.50, 1875: $9.50
107	Guardian (15.5 inches) (Tucker bronze style cast metal dial) – 8D, T&S – 1867, 1869, 1874C, 1876
107	Guardian (15.5 inches) (white [porcelain?] dial) – 8D, T&S – 1874A, 1874B*, 1875 Price: 1874: $11.00, 1875: $11.00
none	Highlander (19.5 inches) – 1D, T&S – 1874A, 1875, 1876 Price: 1875: $7.00
none	Highlander (19.5 inches) – 8D, T&S – 1865, 1867, 1869, 1872, 1874A, 1874B, 1874C, 1875, 1876 Price: 1874: $8.25, 1875: $8.25
none	Horse, Small (14 inches) (same as Parlor in 1865) – 8D, T&S – 1867
	Horse (21 inches) – 8D, T&S – 1865
111B	Horse, B (18 or 18.5 inches) – 8D, T&S – 1869, 1872, 1874A, 1874B, 1874C, 1875, 1876 Price: 1874: $11.25, 1875: $11.25
	Hound (16 inches – 8D, T&S – 1874A, 1874B*, 1875 Price: 1874: $10.50, 1875: $10.50
	Indian Hunter (22 inches) – 8D, T&S – 1880
71A	Innocence (11 inches, lever mvt.) – 1D, T – 1874B*, 1875*, 1876 Price: 1874: $7.00, 1875: $7.00
71A	Innocense (11 inches, lever mvt.) – 1D, T & S – 1874B*, 1875*, 1876 Price: 1875: $7.50, 1875: $7.50
47	Juno (16 or 16.5 inches) – 1D, T&S – 1858, 1865, 1867, 1869, 1872, 1874A, 1874B, 1874C, 1875, 1876 Price: 1874: $1875: $5.75

51	Juno (19 or 19.5 inches) – 8D, T&S – 1858, 1865, 1867, 1869, 1872, 1874A, 1874B, 1874C, 1875, 1876 Price: 1874: $8.25, 1875: $8.25
143	Lady and Child (19 or 20 inches) – 8D, T&S – 1874A, 1874B, 1874C, 1875, 1876 Price: 1874: $15.50, 1875: $15.50
36	Lady Lever (13 inches, lever mvt.) – 1D, T – 1858, 1865, 1867, 1869, 1872, 1874A, 1874B, 1874C, 1875, 1876 Price: 1874: $6.50, 1875: $6.50
36	Lady Lever [or Lady] (13 inches, lever mvt.) – 1D, T&S – 1869, 1874A, 1874B, 1874C, 1875, 1876 Price: 1874: $7.00, 1875: $7.00
36	Lady Lever (13 inches, lever mvt.) – 8D, T – 1858
	Large Horse (see Horse, B.)
52	Leather Stocking (20 inches) – 8D, T&S – 1858
30	Lion Head (15 inches) – 1D, T&S – 1858, 1865, 1867, 1869, 1872, 1874A, 1874B, 1874C, 1875, 1876 Price: 1874: $4.75, 1875: $4.75
30	Lion Head (15 inches) – 8D, T&S – 1875 Price: 1875: $6.00
	Lotos, V. P. (19 inches) – 8D, T&S – 1880
77	Louis XV (18 inches) – 8D, T&S – 1858, 1865, 1867, 1869, 1874A, 1874B*, 1874C, 1876 Price: 1874: $14.50
69	Lovers (17 inches) – 8D, T&S – 1858, 1867
81	Mantel (Mantle) [called Bronze in 1858] (7 inches, lever mvt.) – 1D, T – 1865, 1867, 1869, 1872, 1874A, 1874B, 1874C, 1875, 1876 Price: 1874: $4.75, 1875: $4.75
	Mayflower (15 inches) – 8D, T&S – 1874B, 1874C, 1875, 1876 Price: 1874: $15.00, 1875: $15.00
87	Medallion (13 inches) – 1D & 8D, T&S – 1858
	Mermaid (14.75 inches) – 1D, T – 1867
137	Miner (17.25 or 17 inches) – 8D, T&S – 1874A, 1874B*, 1874C, 1875*, 1876 Price: 1874: $11.25, 1875: $11.25
151	Minerva (12.5 or 13 inches) – 1D, T&S – 1872, 1874A, 1874B, 1875 Price: 1874: $6.00, 1875: $6.00
141	Minerva (15 inches) – 8D, T&S – 1872, 1874A, 1874B, 1874C, 1875, 1876, 1880 Price: 1874: $8.25, 1875: $8.25
	Modern, V. P. (24 inches) – 8D, T&S – 1876

235

Moresque Bronze Lever – 1D – 1869

Moscow (17.25 inches) – 8D, T&S – 1880

Mother and Child (19 inches) – 8D, T&S – 1880

110 Mountaineer (same as Swan, but Mountaineer has figure on top) (20 inches) – 8D, T&S – 1865, 1867, 1869, 1872, 1874A, 1874B*, 1874C, 1875, 1876
   Price: 1874: $14.00, 1875: $14.00

172 Moustache [see No. 34]

Music (21.75 or 22 inches) – 8D, T&S – 1875, 1876, 1880
   Price: 1875: $18.25

Mustang [also called Small Horse, but different from earlier Small Horse] (15 inches) – 8D, T&S – 1867, 1872, 1874A, 1874B, 1874C, 1875, 1876, 1880
   Price: 1874: $7.75, 1875: $7.75

208 Neptune (9 inches) – 8D, T   – 1865, 1867, 1874A, Lever Movement

34 No. 34 [called Mustouche in 1874A & 1874B] (13 inches) – 1D, T – 1858, 1865, 1867, 1869, 1874A, 1874B, 1874C, 1875, 1876
   Price: 1874: $3.50, 1875: $3.50

Novelty, V. P. (24.5 inches) – 8D, T&S – 1876

Oak Leaf (20 inches) – 8D, T&S – 1858, 1865, 1867, 1874A, 1874B*, 1875, 1876
   Price: 1874: $7.00, 1875: $7.00

72 Opera (17 or 18 inches) – 8D, T&S – 1858, 1865, 1867

165 Oriental (17 inches) – 8D, T&S – 1874B*, 1874C, 1875, 1876
   Price: 1874: $8.25, 1875: $8.25

149 Palace (15.5 inches) – 8D, T&S – 1872, 1874A, 1874B, 1874C, 1875, 1876
   Price: 1874: $8.75, 1875: $8.75

Pandora (21 inches) – 8D, T&S – 1880

Parlor (14 inches) (same as Horse, small) – 8D, T&S – 1865

Parlor (10 inches) (different from above, has flat top) – 8D, T&S – 1869, 1872, 1874A, 1874B, 1874C, 1875, 1876
   Price: 1874: $8.75, 1875: $8.75

Parole, V. P. (24 inches) – 8D, T&S – 1880

88 Patchen (19 inches) – 8D, T&S – 1865, 1867, 1869, 1872, 1874A, 1874B*, 1874C, 1875, 1876
   Price: 1874: $15.75, 1875: $15.75

67 Peasant Girl (19 inches) – 1D, T&S – 1874A, 1875*
   Price: 1875: $7.00

67	Peasant Girl (19 inches) – 8D, T&S – 1858, 1867, 1874A, 1875*	
	Price: 1875: $8.25	
	Pen Rack (Penrack, Pen-Rack) (8 inches, lever mvt.) – 1D, T – 1867, 1869, 1874A, 1874C, 1875, 1876	
	Price: 1875: $5.50	
44	Peter and Paul (20 inches) – 8D, T&S – 1858, 1865, 1867, 1869, 1872, 1874A, 1874B, 1874C, 1875*, 1876	
	Price: 1874: $8.75, 1875: $8.75	
161A	Pocahontas (19 or 19.5 inches) – 8D, T&S – 1874A, 1874B*, 1874C, 1875, 1876	
	Price: 1874: $14.50, 1875: $14.50	
	Pompeii (18 or 18.5 inches) – 8D, T&S – 1865, 1867, 1869, 1874A, 1874B*, 1874C, 1875, 1876	
	Price: 1874: $15.75, 1875: $15.75	
165	Oriental (17 inches) – 8D, T&S – 1874A	
	Quail (18 or 19 inches) – 8D, T&S – 1874A, 1874B, 1874C, 1875, 1876	
	Price: 1874: $10.50, 1875: $10.50	
	Ranchero (19 or 20 inches) – 8D, T&S – 1872, 1874A, 1874B, 1874C, 1875, 1876	
	Price: 1874: $15.75, 1875: $15.75	
101	Reaper (18.5 inches) – 8D, T&S – 1865, 1867, 1869, 1872, 1874A, 1874B, 1874C, 1875, 1876, 1880	
	Price: 1874: $14.00, 1875: $14.00	
64	Renaissance (Renaissance) (16 inches) – 1D, T&S – 1865, 1867, 1869, 1872, 1874A, 1874B, 1874C, 1875, 1876	
	Price: 1874: $6.00, 1875: $6.00	
	Rival, V. P. (22 inches) – 8D, T&S – 1876	
	Roccoco (14.5 inches) – 8D, T&S – 1865, 1867	
166	Romance (21 inches) – 8D, T&S – 1874A, 1874B, 1874C, 1875, 1876, 1880	
	Price: 1874: $17.75, 1875: $17.75	
120	Ruin (12.5 inches) – 8D, T&S – 1867, 1869, 1872, 1874A, 1874B, 1875*	
	Price: 1874: $8.25, 1875: $8.25	
	Ruin (18.5 inches) – 8D, T&S – 1874C, 1876	
95	Sailor (17 or 18 inches) – 8D, T&S – 1869, 1872, 1874A, 1874B, 1874C, 1875, 1876	
	Price: 1874: $11.25, 1875: $11.25	
20	Satyr (16 inches) – 8D, T&S – 1858	
	Savoyard (18.5 inches) – 8D, T&S – 1865, 1867, 1869, 1872, 1874A, 1874B, 1874C, 1875*, 1876	
	Price: 1874: $8.75, 1875: $8.75	
66	Scotchman (18 inches) – 8D, T&S – 1858, 1865, 1867, 1869, 1872, 1874A, 1874B, 1874C, 1875, 1876	

11	Scroll (15 inches) – 1D, T&S – 1865, 1869, 1872, 1874B, 1874C, 1875*, 1876	Price: 1874: $8.25, 1875: $8.25 Price: 1874: $4.75, 1875: $4.75
	Sensation (14.75 inches) – 8D, T&S – 1880	
79	Setter (16 or 17 inches) – 8D, T&S – 1858, 1867, 1874A, 1875	Price: 1875: $15.75
	Sentinel, V. P. (18.5 inches) – 8D, T&S – 1880	
	Shanghai (17 inches) – 8D, T&S – 1874A, 1874B, 1874C, 1875, 1876	Price: 1874: $10.00, 1875: $10.00
62	Shepherd Children (17.5 inches) – 1D, T&S – 1858, 1865, 1869, 1872, 1874A, 1874B, 1874C, 1875, 1876	Price: 1874: $7.00, 1875: $7.00
62	Shepherd Children (17.5 inches) – 8D, T&S – 1858, 1865, 1867, 1869, 1872, 1874A, 1874B, 1874C, 1875, 1876	Price: 1874: $8.25, 1875: $8.25
	Sphinx, V. P. (19 inches) – 8D, T&S – 1880	
163	Study (14 inches) – 1D, T&S – 1874A, 1874B, 1874C, 1875	Price: 1874: $6.25, 1875: $6.25
163	Study (14 inches) – 8D, T&S – 1874A, 1874B, 1876	Price: 1874: $7.50
	Superior, V. P. (24 inches) – 8D, T&S – 1876	
110	Swan (same as Mountaineer, but without figure) (13 inches) – 8D, T&S – 1865, 1867, 1869, 1874A, 1874B*, 1874C, 1875*, 1876	Price: 1874: $9.25, 1875: $9.25
	Temple (19.5 inches) – 8D, T&S – 1874B*, 1874C, 1875, 1876	Price: 1874: $18.50, 1875: $18.50
	Trophy (c.15 inches) [without vase] – 8D, T&S – 1869, 1874C, 1876	
	Trophy (18.5 inches) [with vase] – 8D, T&S – 1867, 1869, 1874C, 1876	
147B	Trophy, B. (14.5 inches) [without urn] – 1D, T&S – 1875	Price: 1875: $7.00
147B	Trophy, B. (14.5 inches) [without urn/vase] – 8D, T&S – 1874B*, 1875, 1876	Price: 1874: $8.25, 1875: $8.25
147B	Trophy, B. (c.18 inches) [with urn/vase] – 8D, T&S – 1874B*, 1874C, 1875	Price: 1874: $14.00, 1875: $14.00
167	Ulysses (22.5 inches) – 8D, T&S – 1874A, 1874B, 1874C, 1875, 1876, 1880	

Price: 1874: **$18.25**, 1875: **$18.25**
Unique (13 inches) – 1D, T&S – 1875*, 1876
Price: 1875: **$6.25**
Victor Emmanuel (20 or 20.5 inches) (also called Garabaldi in 1874A) – 8D, T&S – 1872, 1874A, 1874B, 1874C, 1875, 1876
Price: 1874: **$19.00**, 1875: **$19.00**
Victory (14.5 inches) – 1D, T&S – 1872, 1874A, 1874B, 1874C, 1876
Price: 1874: **$6.00**

108V   Vintner (18 or 19 inches) – 8D, T&S – 1865, 1867, 1869, 1874A, 1874B, 1874C, 1875, 1876
Price: 1874: **$9.75**, 1875: **$9.75**
Watch Dogs (13 inches) – 8D, T&S – 1874A, 1875
Price: 1875: **$11.00**

3   Webster (14 or 15 inches) – 8D, T&S – 1853, 1858, 1865, 1867
83   Webster [different from above with man's bust on top] (8 inches) – 1D, T – 1858
116   Wine Drinker (20 inches) – 8D, T&S – 1867, 1869, 1872, 1874A, 1874B, 1874C, 1875, 1876
Price: 1874: **$15.75**, 1875: **$15.75**
Young Navy (18 inches) – 8D, T&S, 1874A

(Castle – shown in Kroeber, must identify. Supposedly 1878.)

INDEX

A
Adam and Eve, 040
Alhambra, 122
Amazon, 152
Amor or Amour, 138
Armorer, 132
Augur, 198
B
Ball Players, 158
Bee, 196
Beggar, 082
Birds, 062
Birds and Cupies, 030
Bird's Nest, 128
Bouquet, 184
Boy and Dog, 098
Boy with Torch, 110
Brady, Matthew, 120
C
Chapel, 174
Chase & Figure, 150
Chase & Pantheon, 088
Cherub and Grapes, 064
Counterpart to Ruin, 148
Cupid (Small), 060
Cupid (Large), 050
D
Dolphin, 066
Dolphin (Clock Stand), 068
Double Statue, 204
Dove, 104
Dragon, 032
E
Eagle, 058
Egyptian, 162, 170, 190
Esmerelda, 116
Etruscan #1, 144
Evangeline, 126
Evangelist, 044
F
Falcon, 134
Fanchon #2, 156
Fisher Boy, 084
Fisher Boy & Dog, 108
Fox and Hare, 074
G
Garland, 090
Gleaner, 140
Globe, 102
Goat, 114
Gothic, 034
Guardian, 124
H
Highlander, 078
I
Indian Hunter, 188
Inkwells, 206
Innocence, 086
J
Juno (Small), 048
Juno (Large), 052
K
Krober, Florence, 016
L
Lady, 042
Lady and Child, 166
Leather Stockings, 056
Lion Head, 036
Louis XV, 092
M
Mantel, 096
Minerva, 164
Morse, Samuel B., 008
Mountaineer, 136
Moustache, 038
Music, 186
N
Neptune, 192
O
Oriental, 178
P
Pallas, 194

Parlor, 054
Patchen, 106
Peasant Girl, 080
Peter and Paul, 046
Pocahontas, 172
Policeman, 200

R
Reaper, 118
Renaissance, 072
Romance, 180
Ruin, 146

S
Sailor, 112
Savoyard, 154
Scotchman, 076
Scroll, 028
Setter, 094

Shepherd Children, 070
Study, 176
Swan (Mountaineer), 136

T
Troubadour, 100

U
Ulysses, 182

V
Victory, 168
Vintner, 130

W
Wall Shelves, 207
Webster, 026
Wine Drinker, 142

A Note from Arlyn

It is my hope that I have given a presence to Nicolas Müller. He has been part of my life for so many years, waiting to be revealed as one of the outstanding figures in American horology.

He has added beauty and innovation to the Art of Clock Making and the ownership of so many of his very unique works of art has brought me great joy. I am delighted to be sharing the information I have been able to accumulate during these forty years. It has been quite an odyssey.

"Honor the Past and Embrace the Future".

ABOUT THE AUTHOR

ARLYN (nee RINGE) RATH was born and educated in the Greater New York area. She has enjoyed dual careers – Kindergarten Teacher and Personal Property Appraiser. (Member of the Appraiser's Association of America).

Very active in The National Association of Watch and Clock Collectors, she was made a Fellow of NAWCC in 1999, after having served as President of New York Chapter #2, as well as its Secretary and Vice-President. Arlyn served as a Committee Chairman in the 2000 Philadelphia National, all of the Greater New York Regionals and one Philadelphia Regional. She has been a speaker at meetings throughout the Northeast and remains on the Executive Council of Chapter #2, writing its Chapter Highlights column for The NAWCC Bulletin.

An avid traveler, along with her husband George, she has visited all seven continents, 161 countries to date, all seven current Wonders of the World and the one remaining Ancient Wonder.

An accomplished needleworker, Arlyn has won numerous awards throughout the country for her work and has raised funds for charities by the donation of some of her original creations. Several articles about her work have appeared in major publications.

Married for more than fifty-five years, she has a daughter, son and four fabulous grandchildren.